PART
ONE

THE BACK

of

THE BUS

FORTY YEARS OF
LEARNING FROM THE POOR

SUSANNE GARNETT

Published in 2020 by Ryeford Press

Copyright © Susanne Garnett

First Edition

The rights of Susanne Garnett to be identified as the
author of this work has been asserted in accordance with
the Copyright, Designs and Patents Act, 1988.

ISBN   978-1-64871-025-4

Cover Design by 100Covers.com
Interior Design by FormattedBooks.com

Contents

Part Four

Introduction
What the grass told the elephants

This book is about the mystery of human existence, which you might justifiably say is a rather ambitious topic. But it is also a book about very small things, forgotten people, discarded sweaters, and frozen fingers wrapped around mugs of tea, tiny babies lying on mud floors, and dancing till dawn.

It is mainly an account of the conversations I have been able to have with many people who live in places all round the world, both on and off the beaten tracks. Many of them are far beyond the sharp end, below the lowest of safety nets, way up those creeks where you would never wish to go, even with a paddle. It is a book of stories about those girls and boys, women and men who have taken the scant grains of nourishment offered to them and turned them into glory.

It is also about the paradox of poverty. It is in part about angels, and miracles, and righteous anger. It is also about grace and gifts. It is certainly not a treatise about religion, organised or otherwise. I hope it is about honesty, and humanity, and in places, humour.

As the eighteenth-century wordsmith, Dr Johnson, once said, "I too have tried to be a philosopher, but cheerfulness would keep breaking in." So, I do hope this is a cheerful book, rather than a philosophical tract. I was once trained as a historian, now I am simply someone who likes to observe, and record, and sit with people to have a laugh.

All my life, I have struggled to understand why in such a beautiful world so many people suffer and die horrible deaths at the hands of their uncaring and often vindictive fellow humans. Why next to a billionaire's mansion, a woman can die in childbirth crouched under a cardboard box, why tiny children have to crush stones or carry bricks to build palaces for people who scarcely acknowledge their existence.

But there is also the inescapable truth, that it is so often those who have nothing to speak of, neither fame or wealth, beauty, good health, or even talent, who give us the clearest of messages about the meaning of our lives.

That is not to say I have come up with any definitive answers. The opposite in fact. In some ways, it is just a collection of other people's stories, along with a few of my own. To frame it, I have had to give an account of my own wanderings round the world, and forty-five years spent mainly in the "aid" sector, but I do hope this book is not all about my life. It is far more about the hundreds of people I have met on the way, who have been wonderful messengers about what it is to be a human being.

In many parts of the world I have travelled, either in overcrowded mini-buses, or Filipino "jeepneys", or in the beaten little white pick-ups used by the poorest agencies in Africa. The view from the back of these buses, where you can see and taste the dust you have thrown up behind you, and hear the conversations around you, often gives the truest record of what is really going on in the world. It is in such circumstances that I have often learned the most.

It is not uncommon these days to hear people say you shouldn't tell other people's stories, and that you should remain culturally quarantined within your own immediate life experience, but if that is the case, how impoverished we would all be. I am sure Shakespeare never experienced his uncle killing his father, or knew what it was like to be a Prince of Denmark. Lucy Montgomery wasn't herself raised in the same poverty as her creation, Anne of Green Gables, (though she did live with pretty austere elderly relations).

Of course, I do understand what the objectors mean by cultural colonialism. History of the hunt is usually written by the hunters, after all. But for many of the people whose stories I have tried to share, no-one will ever hear their stories from their own mouths. Their voice and their agency have been denied them, and many of them have died.

I also believe, turning this argument on its head, sometimes we are blinded to our own stories as well, when we are simply too close to them. Our vision is blurred, sometimes by our tears, it must be said, but also, sometimes by those glasses we learn to put on at an early age, to cope with passions and anxieties swirling within our families which we cannot understand or deal with. But the power of story, and its ability to liberate is profound. There are surely few more important roles in a tribe or a culture than that of the storyteller.

CHAPTER

1

A World of Words and Water
1957 Gloucestershire, England

I was born in England in the early 1950s, the child of frustrated working-class people who were bright enough to go to university, but were stopped, by economic necessity, by the Second World War, and by the cultural limitations of their time and place. This meant, like many others, I was sometimes encouraged by my parents to develop ambitions they could not realise for themselves, merged with ideas ridiculously big for my boots.

I also inherited a huge restlessness, a need to take wings and fly far, far away. And yet I knew I carried a heritage of story, my own, my parents', and that of their ancestors. From the beginning, I carried this weight of other people's words, of their life stories, with me.

These stories are luggage I can never abandon, and as I have grown older, and family history has become more accessible, I have added several bundles more: knowledge of my father's equally unusual, equally poverty-stricken forebears, who can be traced back to Ireland, and the West Cork home of the

McCarthys, where the most famous bearers of the name built Blarney Castle, home of the famous stone which legend says gives the gift of the gab.

And behind the Irish, lie the bones of the Vikings, the Angles and the Saxons, the Romans, and those generations of Celts and ancient peoples who recognised the landscapes we know today as their very own. We all share this heritage in Britain. None of us is special. Each of us is unique.

I was born in 1952 in a steep Gloucestershire valley, where the West Country accents were strong and pervasive. I still have not lost the traces of mine to this day. Our town of Stroud wasn't at all fashionable then, or especially attractive. It had as much red brick as golden Cotswold stonework, and was dominated by the woollen mills, some of which had been turned into small engineering works.

These throbbing old buildings, originally using the waters of the River Frome and the rain which poured down the valleys to power their looms, had provided work for eight generations of men and women who used to tramp up to ten miles to go through their gates at seven in the morning, or seven at night.

It was a world born out of damp, of fragrant mould and mosses ripped from the derelict mill-yard walls. It was a country bound by green silence, broken only by the rain trickling down deep-set cottage windows. A sly fertility lurked everywhere, breeding the steep clutter of the little town of Stroud, the place where I was born, and my heart's first clumsy home.

I came, like many a Gloucestershire child, from a family running like unravelled wool through the valleys, loose-knitted into a web of cheerful enmity. Men and women of

Chalford, Nailsworth, Thrupp, breathed the damp silence and lived on its produce of consumptive intelligence. They were born in leaking attics, crowded into picturesque slums, whose charms grew with the invention of the damp-course, and clambered like weeds out of the steep banks. I will always remember the smell of that damp, sitting in the wide window seat of my grandfather's cottage, reading his books of sermons.

My forefathers, now sunk under overgrown chapel willow-herb in unmarked graves, were all talkers, preachers, liars. In the damp literary climate their wits tended to bolt and they often ended up too bright for their own good. Those who didn't turn to crime, stayed poor, grew flint-shouldered for the better bearing of grudges and would stalk for miles in search of a decent row. They were proud, articulate and contentious, able to fling an opinion as far as Gloucester.

They were sometimes gifted poets, their pedigree lost in an oblivion of argument, but they could also be rude, coarse and inclined to run away from responsibility. This is proven by the number of my grandparents and great-grandparents, on both sides, who had unknown male parentage.

Words could be as frothy as elder, as sharp as the wild garlic, or as gold and deep as the wide-cupped marigolds. Under the grey beech trees, the woods rang with the fertile literacy, echoed back from the classrooms, permeating the valleys with song.

When I was seven, I started at the Black Boy School at the top of Castle Street. It was a strange name for a girls' primary school. But a small bronze figure of an African child gave it its name. The figure was part of a rare Jack Clock; a clock with a black figure which turned to strike a bell on the hour.

The black figure, or jack, about two feet high, was

described by a nineteenth century local historian, Fisher, as "turning his head, lifting his club, and striking the hours of day and night as they came round." The statue had been cast back in 1774, and had been moved from its original place outside a watchmakers, first to the front of one of Stroud's many pubs, the Duke of York, halfway up the town, until finally being elevated to Castle Street School. Stroud had a proud, radical history of opposition to the slave trade, and the early mill workers had rallied in support of emancipation.

The Black Boy school, housed in the 1844 stone building, sadly closed the year after I left, first to become a teacher's centre, then, inevitably, eventually sold to developers who turned it into flats. But its very stones must surely still re-echo the thousands of words we learned and recited, sang and shouted in and out of its lofty classrooms, with their large pot-bellied coke stoves.

I suppose the school was somewhat of an anachronism, even then. The stone stairs had been worn away in the middle by countless children's feet running up and down them for more than a century.

Every Thursday afternoon we would stand, a hundred little girls in our smocked cotton dresses and Clark's sandals and sing the ancient songs, incantations flung out through the open casements across the sun-dusted valley.

We were taught Shakespearean songs as rich and incomprehensible as Latin, doxying many an innocent dale, songs from the past, by William Blake and Thomas Arne, all learned by rote and never forgotten. Our headmistress then, who retired the year we left, epitomised the power of an articulate Gloucestershire brain. She too was just a little crazy.

Dear Miss Peacock – as fierce and as unpredictable as Rumpelstiltskin.

"Guess my middle name." she would challenge us, barelegged and jacketless, even in December. "Guess my middle name."

It turned out to be Ridley, though none of us solved the riddle. Then she would show us her scars.

"See. Look. That's where my brother threw the skissors at me. Always call them skissors, girls. Then you'll remember the 'c'!"

We stared at her strong naked arms in fear, as she spun our straw-stuffed minds into gold. By the time we reached her class, however, we were already drenched with words, having learned long passages of the 1662 Authorised Version of the Bible by heart.

"Tell it not in Gath," I would stoutly order my small brother at the age of ten. "Publish it not in the streets of Ashkelon, lest the daughters of the Philistines rejoice, lest the daughters of the uncircumcised triumph." At school we had just learned David's lament over the death of Saul and Jonathan from the Old Testament.

This was heady stuff indeed, which left us dazed and endowed me ever after with a fatal attraction and fascination for long words. I had no idea, of course, of half what I was saying. We were also read aloud to, right up to the age of eleven, and that was how I became acquainted with Kipling's *Jungle Book*, *Great Expectations*, and *Treasure Island*, which we turned into a puppet show. Characters like Magwitch, and Ben Gunn, lonely and desperate, entered my consciousness and never left it.

Many women in Stroud may remember Miss Peacock, her

sewing classes, the mulberry tree with its silkworms, her green ink, and her strange insistence that one sheet of toilet paper was enough for all purposes. We told our parents about her vigorous eccentricities, but I don't think they really believed us.

But I told no-one of the magic place I found at the end of the sports' field which guaranteed four-leaved clovers. I would wander there, moving further and further back from a Rounders' game, under the guise of fielding, and then quietly lie down to sleep until the game was over. I wonder if those clovers are still there, or maybe only their memory remains, the magical genetic diversity lost under bulldozers' oblivious churning of the soil to build yet more houses.

After school, in the summer months I would walk alone the two miles home back up to Rodborough across the canal. The walk took me under the cavernous viaduct, and then for a long steep climb up through the sorrel-sprinkled hayfields, picking lady's smocks or cuckoo-pint as I went.

No one bothered me, or tried to control these life-giving rambles. No parents ever accompanied us to the school. Winter and summer, we would walk there, two or three children at a time, or alone, first down one long steep hill, and then up another, right through the town centre. I don't ever remember my mother even visiting the school for a conference. It would have been considered an unusual and shocking thing if she had.

They were years of freedom and security, those late Fifties of my childhood. My father even took me for piano lessons on the back of his motorbike without a helmet. He wore a gabardine mackintosh coat, and I felt perfectly secure tucking my music case inside his belt, and then just holding onto it as I perched behind him. My parents only bought a car some years later. Like the television, and the fridge, it was a strange and exciting addition to our domestic economy, and it took a while for us to get used to having it.

In the winter, the walk was inevitably even longer, as cutting down through the fields would result in drenched clothes and sodden shoes. We would stick to the roads and enjoy the various smells, the heady malt coming from the brewery, the nasty smell from the great ballooning canister of gas.

There was a penny sometimes given for the bus, but we normally spent that at the baker's shop opposite the school. We were all addicted to the soft little white rolls the baker would save for us, and exchange for a large flat coin.

As the years changed, so did the way home, as my parents moved house when my father joined the Fire Brigade, and needed to live within a mile of the Fire Station. Many nights I would run down the wide cobbled lane past Strachan's Mill, which made cloth for billiard tables, and which was reputed originally to have produced the bright scarlet cloth for the British army until the end of the nineteenth century. I used to play with friends who lived beyond the eponymously named Murder Lane which had seen a young girl bludgeoned to death a century earlier.

We would lean over the parapet of the grey stone bridge and watch the dappled trout dart under the brown water. The lime trees dripped, their leaves delightful to dissect with our small hands revealing their tracery, and alarming shafts of steam would rise up at us above the moss-covered pipes. All around us, day and night rang the never-ceasing crash of the looms.

We would make nests of moss, leaving them hopefully

in the branches of young tree in case the birds took up the offer. But the wheeling swallows and martins, cutting the air with their neat little tails, seemed far more inclined to perch uncomfortably under the eaves of the old mill building, digesting the clouds of gnats which hovered over the river.

"And did those feet?" we sang, as we felt the cobbles slip under our sandals, and we watched the rain splash into circles of light as they hit the water. Of course, they did. It was a world of words and water, the essential gift of God's creation, our own Eden. We even had our own dark satanic mills!

CHAPTER
2

Pursuing Angels
1960 My English roots

I didn't start out as a religious maniac. In fact, my earliest memories of all matters to do with God were completely negative, starting with a hellish experience in Religious Education. I have always taken a dim view of Sunday schools, ever since my youthful excursions into the gloomy basement schoolrooms of our local Baptist Church.

My father had been wooed into its fellowship by the camaraderie of the male voice choir and my mother compromised her Congregationalist principles by giving in both to the choir and someone else's notion that I should attend the Sunday school.

I owed my enrolment there to the stern encouragement of its superintendent who lived opposite us and who marshalled his own children down the hill there every week. I remember one Sunday afternoon in 1957 screaming with rage for the entire two-mile walk, the elastic of my green felt hat digging into my chin and the scratchy, sugar-stiffened petticoat rubbing against my knees.

For a long time after, my mental picture of Oliver Twist picking oakum (whatever that was) was firmly set in those Baptist cellars. We seemed always to be weaving raffia with spiky needles which pricked your fingers badly. This led to an inevitable fight with the girl on the next stool to decide who could grab the few un-splintered strands.

This workhouse environment was only enlivened, if that is the word, by the faded, framed 'cradle-roll' pictures of a blue-eyed, effeminate Jesus in his white nightie, surrounded by little white babies, cuddling up, and little black babies, kneeling down at the front. I immediately warmed to the little black babies more than the sissy white ones.

The light must have been very poor, because I distinctly remember taking absolutely literally the words of the old chorus, "Jesus bids us shine," and wondering sadly why my small corner was so very gloomy. Eventually, either I was chucked out of the Sunday school, or my parents finally decided not to make every Sunday a re-run of the Battle of Waterloo, (I can't quite remember which), but on my release from the cellar experience I do remember vowing never to wear the horrible green felt hat ever again. And I never did.

When I was nine, we moved away from the censorious gaze of the Baptist Superintendent to another section of the town, and encountered a different style of evangelism from the kindly local vicar, Mr Roberts. The very day we were moving in, he called in on his bicycle with an uncomplicated word of greeting and ended up staying for a cup of tea and a slice of fruitcake.

He helped us unpack the several tea chests littering the front lawn, and when he finally pushed his bike down the front path and cycled off, he gave my mother a copy of the parish magazine and an assurance that should we choose, we would always be welcome at the little daughter church along the road.

This encounter kept my mother as a notional Anglican for the rest of her eighty-nine years, although she was always too proud to admit she had never been confirmed in the Church of England, and simply pretended she had been. This little fib never bothered anyone else, and I am sure it never caused the Almighty to raise a figurative eyebrow.

So, we started to attend this Anglican Church, much more formal than the Baptists, and without the thundering sermons or raffia mat making of the previous denominations. After a year or so, I joined the Choir and delved into sixteenth-century language again with great enthusiasm for the *Book of Common Prayer* Evensong services. I learned to sing pointed Psalms and the Mag and Nunc, as we called them, and recognised the same psalms and Bible passages I had read and learned in my primary school.

Mine was very much a cultural Christianity. I had been given the training. I knew the hymns. And it has stayed with me all my life, even though I have walked the ways of many different religions, and certainly surveyed the gamut of many strange versions of Christianity.

But when I was eight, I had my future career clearly planned out, and I would be certainly multi-skilled and flexible in my approach. I had read in the Children's Encyclopaedia, twenty volumes of which formed the bottom shelf of our bookcase, all about the story of David Livingstone. And it had fired my imagination.

I decided I wanted to be a missionary in Africa and my ambitions centred round little black babies, just like the ones on the Sunny Smiles booklets we were given in Sunday school. I remember saying to my bemused parents that I would, "teach them in the morning, run a hospital in the afternoon and hold services in the evening."

This self-confidence in both my abilities and the world's need for my efforts sustained me for a long time. In a crazy sort of way I suppose my life has followed its course along somewhat not dissimilar lines. Most of my various jobs and attempts at what one might call a career in international development, can in some way be traced back to the religious enthusiasms and curiosity of my childhood.

There is a universal human urge to see something beyond the law of the jungle and the survival of the most powerful. When I was nine, (having moved on from wanting to be a missionary, but still religious), I decided I really wanted to see an angel. This was probably because I had read a book about Joan of Arc, and had also seen Jennifer Jones in a film about Bernadette of Lourdes on our newly acquired TV.

Not being raised Catholic, I didn't pitch as far or as high as the Virgin Mary of course, but I invented my own lovely angel. I knew he would be waiting in all his feathers and glory if I could just get up to the tin-roofed chapel at the end of our street, and catch him when the church was empty.

Of course, I never ventured up to the church building, apart from Sunday evenings when I sang in the choir for the evening service, and I knew he wouldn't be there, then, not in public. But I held him in my heart, for a long time, and imagined him there, in the corrugated tin church as I cycled past on my evening paper-round.

But then, he was very much an angel of my childhood, and I am now the other side of middle-aged, and certainly no longer a child. He was also male, which I took for granted in those days. I don't think he would be today.

However, without a doubt I have certainly met angels.

They have not been at all like the feathered friend of my childhood fantasies. But they have been magnificent, they have been all shapes and sizes of people, old and very young, and they have almost without exception been people who have struggled on the edge of survival. The ones I have actually encountered have been those people who have given me strange, illusive insights into how the infinite mysteries of our existence can be understood in human terms.

So, these angels, these messengers, have walked into the life I was privileged to be given and they have fed me with their stories, their realities. Some of their stories have been tragic, some horrific, and others very lovely. But they have all shared something which doesn't always come easily to us today. The stories are all true in the sense that they are not fantasy. And I have tried my best to tell them truthfully as well.

As the sunny uplands of childhood inevitably changed into the angst laden but fascinating world of an intense adolescence my world was dominated by the structures and personalities of my girls' grammar school. I adored the smell of the new leather satchels we all had to buy, the exotic treasures of new worlds open to us through studying French, and Latin, even the ridiculous and petty school rules. I was once given a C for a perfectly correct essay because I had not underlined the title.

But my teachers were mainly appallingly snobbish, and I spent a good deal of energy openly challenging them. I remember once organising a bus load of children in wheelchairs from the nearest special school to come to one of our school concerts. And when we had mock elections at the time of the

Wilson government, I stood as the Labour candidate, losing of course, as it was Labour policy to abolish grammar schools.

By the time I was fifteen I knew I wanted to read history, which pleased my teachers, and I also persuaded the school to offer World Affairs as an AO level, although the teacher they gave us prepared nothing and simply read us snippets from the Times she filched from the staff-room.

In my early teens I had started to travel, firstly with my parents on a bus-trip to Belgium and the Netherlands, and then to Switzerland by the same means. These were very exciting, except that my mother refused to eat meat any way other than burned to a crisp, and embarrassed us all by complaining about deliciously soft and pink slices of beef. She also had a panic attack at the top of the Grindalwald open-chair ski lift, and jumped off her seat just as we took off.

As I sailed down the valley alone in my little swinging chair, I realised for the first time, that adults were not the solid rock they were made out to be. This somehow was a very liberating thought. Poor mother had a two-mile downward hike to meet up with me again, and was completely ashamed of herself, but I was completely calm. I had enjoyed the peace and relief from the constant soundtrack of her nervous criticisms of every new experience we encountered.

Once my French improved slightly I also spent several weeks each August going as a general help with my great aunt to Normandy, where she rented a villa and exposed the prep-school children she taught to a bit of foreign culture. But it was when I was in the final term of my school career, the third year sixth, where a small group of us were the female equivalent of Alan Bennett's "History Boys," that my horizons really opened. I had the chance to go to America.

American High Schools in those days operated, as many may still do, a scheme of running exchange programmes which brought students from all over the world to study in the USA for the junior year, (or for students from the UK usually for pupils in the first year of the sixth form). You lived with an American family, and attended public high school, along with the host family's offspring, who became your host brother or sister.

My head mistress, whose niece at Cheltenham Ladies College had managed to get one of these scholarships, decided I should put in for one, and wrote me a positive reference. I think she could see how desperate I was to get away.

Our joint application was successful and I was given the huge privilege of a year in America funded by the Quaker foundation of the American Field Service. Once the dreaded Oxbridge exams and interviews were over, I travelled to the States from an exceptionally bleak British winter in 1970, into the luxury of Southern California.

Cultural diversity was encouraged in those days. My travelling companions included a Jewish girl from North London who became part of a large black family living in Oakland.

She was the only daughter of elderly Orthodox parents, and went to live with a black Roman Catholic family. Her American "Dad" was a butcher by trade, and the kids were all bussed across the city to a largely white middle-class High School. Within a month or two, she completely identified with her black family, and was never the same again. I met her again at the end of the year and she said to me, "I feel black now. Whenever I see black people, I think they are my folk, my family. I feel we belong together."

This was what the most idealistic people running the scheme had hoped to achieve, the widening of empathies, and a greater tolerance of diversity, by not only walking a mile in someone else's moccasins, but also sharing them on a permanent basis. Children of host families generally followed suit by travelling themselves to study in various other countries. My host sister had already been to Finland for a semester.

We flew in initially into New York, and were housed in a hostel very close to the United Nations Building. I remember being completely over-awed by the height of the sky-scrapers, and by the accents of everyone. They were just so . . so . . American!

I realised I had come to a completely different continent and I had better get used to it.

We had a day of induction and then flew on again to our various destinations. I came down from the skies six hours later or so, into the benign warmth of Southern California, and, astonished by the 30 degree rise in temperature from New York, began hastily to unwind my long woollen scarf and undo the buttons on my turquoise maxi-coat even as I walked from the plane.

Los Angeles International Airport assaulted my eyes with unexpected contrasts everywhere I looked. I remember it was carpeted in a pleasant pale blue colour, unheard of in Europe at that time. The roads, and the cars packed onto them all looked enormous, the traffic-lights dangled from precariously swinging loose wires.

But my host family was there to collect me in the Arrivals hall, and that was the main thing. It was two days and nights since I had left Gloucestershire, and I was more than ready to see them.

Faced with an intense, opinionated gabby young English student, whose vocabulary and accent they found hard to understand, my host family tried very hard. I tried hard too, but we weren't a fit made in heaven, despite all the vetting procedures of the American Field Service volunteer placement officers.

The family into which I dropped were staunchly Republican, very Masonic in all their social activities and friends, and apparently Presbyterian. Dad was the manager of a Company Credit Union, and a keen fisherman.

A kindly soul, who had emigrated west from Georgia as a young man and still retained his Southern accent, he followed his wife's opinions on everything. She worked as a medical technician, helping a local doctor with all the blood tests and specimen collection in his surgery. When I lived with them in the affluent suburban city of Whittier, I eventually grew fond of them, but the culture shock was profound.

They had just one daughter, who had been born when her parents were both well into their middle-age, and was a classic only child. Told she had to share her bedroom with me, she was less than enthralled. I was astonished that she had her own car to drive to school most days, and the teen culture within Southern California both entranced me by its 'otherness', and also puzzled me with its vapidity.

The High School had no uniform, but nearly every day my host sister wore a uniform for a different activity or sorority, and in the odd days between, there was an agony of choice as to what to wear. It seemed anathema to wear the same outfit two days running, or even twice in the same week. My slim wardrobe would face an extreme challenge, a problem I kept to myself.

But there was no secrecy attached to the Masonic activities. Dad, who was about sixty-five when I stayed with them, was deeply proud of his masonic connections, and showed me all his books of rubric and told me just what they did in lodge ceremonies. My American Mom went to the women's equivalent meetings, called the Eastern Star, and my host sister, a very serious, careful sort of girl when it came to making new friends, was a member of Job's Daughters, the girls' section, where they dressed bizarrely in long flowing white robes and like in her parents' groups, had to learn the ceremonial verses off by heart. I thought they were all bananas, and said so.

They did show me great kindness and generosity during the eight months I lived with them, but their world view could not have been more different from mine. I especially remember having battles royal with them over the Vietnam War, which was in full flood at the time.

June, my American 'Mom', in particular pressed all the wrong buttons in me, and I was once so angry I broke a plate which I was washing in the kitchen sink. She referred to the Vietcong as "yellow savages who should all be killed. They don't feel love or pain like we do." Her daughter, my host sister would roll her eyes and dismiss these comments, but I could barely tolerate them.

But June was very much a child of her own culture, brought up by a rigid Presbyterian grandmother in 1920s Los Angeles. Her mother had run off with a notorious gangster with a name so famous, that one of the city's main boulevards still remains named after him. June had had a very lonely childhood as a result.

I eventually learned to hold my tongue. Our community was completely middle-class, but I soon joined up with a group of far more radical High School friends, and began to feel less of a fish out of water. Then I realised my education had only just begun.

CHAPTER

3

A Doll Bigger than a Child
1970 USA and Mexico

The train you ride through life will take you where you never expected to go. This happened to me in Tijuana, in Northern Mexico, back in December of 1970 when I was eighteen. In my very first week in California, the leaders of a girls' sorority group from my host high school invited me to join them on a field trip.

"It'll be such fun," they said. "We're taking a bus down across the border into Mexico for a day trip, to give a party down for some kids in a mission. We have collected gifts to distribute for them, and we have a ton of food."

I was still reeling from the opulence and razzamatazz of a Californian pre-Christmas shopping festival of light. Plastic reindeer hung from the palm trees alongside the road leading from the airport, and everyone seemed to decorate the outside, rather than the inside of their houses.

These days it is more commonplace to see external Christmas decorations in the UK but in Britain of 1970, with constant electricity black-outs, I had seen nothing like it. I thought I had gone to some sort of plastic Nirvana, where electricity was virtually free, and all the sixteen and seventeen-year-old students in my school drove huge cars. One of the girls in my group even had her own Porsche.

So we set off, in one of the many school district buses, laden with cakes and cookies, canned drinks of soda, and hundreds of lovely toys donated by generous parents. Then as we crossed the border, the weather changed. A cold wind blew, and clouds settled over the coast, laden with moisture. It was damp, foggy and depressing.

Tijuana, fifty years ago, was very much a border town, but relied on tourism, especially providing facilities for the swollen military population of the San Diego naval bases and San Clemente barracks. It was the height of the Vietnam War, and one definitely felt the military presence.

The centre of the city had plenty of Mexican themed restaurants, bright with red and green bunting and festive cheer, but where we were heading was way off the beaten track to an area I later recognised as a typical favela, rickety patched up houses on a self-build basis, clinging to the steep slopes of a canyon, without paint, or pretty lights, and no plastic reindeer in sight. A harassed looking nun, dressed in a sweatshirt and stained black skirt, greeted us with relief, as the bus splashed to a standstill.

We unloaded our instant party as the sudden sharp rainstorm soaked us and we saw the fifty or so children waiting outside the hall, ragged, cold and hungry. One of the first things I noticed was that up to a third of these little Mexicans were blonde and blue eyed and looked uncannily like the younger siblings of my school mates, except these were undersized, dirty and looked definitely malnourished. Many were barefooted.

Even I, in my naivety, could see that they were the living by-product of the military personnel's rest and recreational activities south of the US/Mexican border. Collateral damage perhaps, from a careless refusal by the guys to take responsibility for sexual proclivities, or even to wearing a condom.

The next thing I learned, which really shook me to the core, was that the community hall was situated on a hill actually under a cemetery, and the flooding had opened many of the graves, so the effluent, even including some bones, ran down the canyon road in front of its door. No-one seemed to think this was an appalling health issue.

The organisers of the party locked the children out in the rain until we had put up the decorations and laid out the party food. Then we let them inside. They poured through the door, but then stood in silence. It was unnerving to say the least.

None of the children were laughing. They looked at us solemnly in shy and bewildered silence, but all the boys automatically lined up in front of all the girls, and the bigger boys pushed their way straight to the front. We had laid out iced cakes, and drinks, and they were demolished within minutes. Then we distributed the presents.

The boys grabbed the best ones first and then began to fight among themselves. I helped on the girls' line, and passed out various pink boxes, and themed toys. Then I was handed an especially tall, beautifully dressed doll about three feet high to give to a child.

This doll had blonde curls and big blue eyes which blinked. On her plastic feet were nice cotton socks and buckled shoes, and under her pretty dress were proper little panties.

The child approaching me to receive this gift, little Maria, was probably about six years old, but looked no bigger than a British three-year-old. She was smaller than the doll, and weighed almost less. Unlike the toy, she had no such socks and shoes. In fact, she had no underwear at all, just a skimpy shift dress.

In a state of shock, I handed over the doll to her and we stared at each other in one of those cosmic moments when the points change. Mutual incomprehension of what she should do with the doll seemed to connect us. She looked at me, then looked at the doll. Then she summoned all her strength and struggled to carry it away. All I could do was hope she made it home somehow, and that her mother would be able to strip off the doll's clothes and put them on her.

This little incident, from one day in my life as an exchange student, was to stay with me for ever. One incident, but it was to be the first of very many encounters on the long learning curve I needed to take, to make any sense of what life is all about.

The gifted high school teacher who took me along on the Mexican trip, also arranged a visit to Watts Towers in a corner of South Los Angeles where my host family would never visit, to see one man's outstanding contribution to American art. Seventeen architectural features including a set of connected towers which rise almost to 100 feet, dominate the local landscape.

In 1921, Sabato Rodia, an Italian immigrant, had started to build them in his own small building lot, in the city of Watts next to the railway tracks, just in his spare time from his work as a building labourer.

For the next thirty years he worked, mainly using scrap

pieces of steel, covered in mesh like chicken wire, and then plastered with cement, and daily risking his life, as he could not afford proper scaffolding. Sabato was never trained as more than a building labourer but he was an eccentric genius, and his towers still stand to this day.

When I visited, and marvelled at the amazing construction, the city of Watts had become a mainly Black area, as African-Americans had been pushed out of other areas of Los Angeles, and it was considered rough. Those who were too scared even to visit the site didn't know what they were missing. Now, at least, they are seen as a vital part of California's cultural heritage.

With teachers and other generous folk, I also visited China Town, and explored the diversity of Los Angeles' heritage. The Mission stations still stand in various coastal resorts and university campuses, but there is so much left untold. I went to Catalina Island and heard the sad story of the demise of the local Native tribes, and also into Arizona to visit Hopi villages and admire the sand paintings and other artwork. But the people who made these richly symbolic pictures and artefacts, where were they? They seemed very elusive. It was mid- summer, before I realised where most of them had gone, those who survived. They had headed for the hills.

The July 4th weekend in 1971 was very special for me. I will always remember the date, because I spent it with a Navaho – Apache family high in the remote forests of southern New Mexico, at a proper Pow-Wow. There were many tribes represented there, with names mostly unknown to me, and most people were dressed, sometimes in part, sometimes fully, in traditional Native American costumes. More than a hundred tee-pees, made from hide or canvas round a tripod or long wooden poles were erected into a temporary city, unlike any I had so far seen in the United States.

I sat on a grassy bank watching the show, and next to me was a man dressed in a resplendent costume of white suede fringed jacket and trousers, laden with silver and turquoise jewellery, and wearing a full-length feather headdress. He looked amazingly like a legendary Indian chief from the old story books.

He seemed perfectly content to share his space with a young red-headed white girl, but I was far too shy in that instance to talk to him. We sat together on the bank and I could almost feel the meeting of our completely separated cultures.

The moonlight eventually faded, as did the brightest of the stars, and a soft pale blue dawn began to creep up the eastern sky. Reluctantly, as the drumming finally stopped and the exhausted dancers collapsed into a heap of sleeping bodies, the gathering, the pow-wow, drew to a close.

I should explain how I arrived there. My time in the USA had given me many more distinctive experiences of different cultures, but this encounter happened towards the end of the trip.

As exchange students in California we were gathered together from across the Southland and loaded on to buses to be given a pilgrimage through the heartland of old America. The plan was that we should be taken to meet people and see different US communities just for one or two nights, to which our main hosts may not have been able or thought necessary to expose us.

Our bus started in Orange County and moved off towards its first stop, due east from Los Angeles, across the desert to

Yuma, famous for its now closed notorious gaol and where you could literally fry eggs on the pavement. People ran from air-conditioned houses straight through a blistering oven of the outside air into their air-conditioned cars. How the native population of Pima Native Americans sitting out under the sequoia cactus trees coped with the heat I could not fathom.

In the one night we were in Yuma I went on a date with a young man from Greece, a previous exchange student stranded in exile while his country fought the Turks and battled against fascist generals who had enacted a coup in his absence. He worked for a farmer locally and was full of fun.

My host family in Yuma were pleased I accepted his invitation to drink Pepsi and watch the moon rise over the desert.

"He gets lonesome, because of course none of the local girls are allowed to date him."

"Why ever not?"

"He's a foreigner of course."

That was Yuma, but the best adventure was yet to come.

Our large bus meandered on out of Arizona into New Mexico, and at the pick-up point in Santa Fe, the local organiser came over and said she was going to ask me a favour. Because I was a native English speaker, and one of the older students, nineteen instead of seventeen, would I agree to stay with a Native American family who lived someway from town, and who were the first ever to ask for a student house guest for the weekend?

Of course, I jumped at the opportunity, and went back home with the folks she beckoned across. They were articulate, intelligent and highly reflective people. Mom was Navaho and taught in the Indian High School on a reservation. Dad was

Apache, a physicist at Los Alamos research facility, and his father also lived with them, in his own adobe house at the end of their compound.

They lived ten miles out of Santa Fe, up the winding dust roads, and into an area on the edge of a reservation, which looked exactly like a film set for a Hollywood Western. You could almost hear the old wooden doors banging in the wind and see the livery stable, waiting to change horses for the noon hour stagecoach skidding with its galloping horses round the canyon roads.

The grandfather was also a reincarnation of the old days in the South West. He was a pure ethnic Apache, spoke no English and had been born in the 1880s. He remembered the 100-mile forced marches and ethnic cleansing of that period. He could have filled a book for me, but sadly we could not converse.

Instead he fashioned me a silver rabbit with a turquoise stone as a brooch. I kept it and wore it for years until the clasp wore out and I lost it somewhere, to my eternal regret.

His son, the father of the family, had work which was classified so he could not talk about it, which meant that our conversation was again somewhat limited. The family members I mostly talked to were their two younger sons, ridiculously good-looking boys, one a Junior and his brother a sophomore in the local high school. They had shiny, almost navy-blue hair which they wore very long, right down their backs below their shoulder blades.

"Why is your hair like that?" (I was usually never shy of asking personal questions.)

"For film work. All summer we will get jobs as stunt riders and extras for the Hollywood westerns which are made out here. It pays really well. Come on, we'll go down to the river to catch some horses and we'll show you."

"Don't you get angry having to play traditional stereotyped Red Indians?"

"Nah. The pay's too good. We're saving for college."

We went down at dawn to the nearest creek the next morning, which was when their horses came to drink and were close enough to catch. The boys seemed to be able to magically summon their favourites out of the herd, slipping a rope over their necks and riding them bareback without bridles up towards me.

Then they put on a little show for me, galloping back and forth, sliding down the side of the horses as if to hide from gunfire, performing instant stops, twirls, and even somersaults from one horse to the other. They were magnificent horsemen.

After half an hour or so of these games, they released the horses back into the wild, and laughingly we returned to the house. The younger boy showed me his ducklings. He had a clutch of about twelve and was raising them around a wash bowl.

"Beginnings of my ranch," he explained.

But I also learned of the challenges facing this original American family. The oldest son, who had hoped to be at university that year had instead been drafted, and was now serving in Vietnam. Native American youths were drafted at a higher proportion than almost any other sector of society. He knew he stood no chance of deferment or escaping military service. Anxiety about the war in the Far East clouded all the family's happiness.

On the July 4th weekend, it was time for a spectacular gathering they wanted me to see. We loaded the old station wagon and set off, a hundred miles or more south up into the forests of New Mexico. The white folks' towns disappeared as the trees grew thicker, and I noticed many other vehicles, all loaded with tepee poles and various items of camping gear, carrying large families, headed in the same direction as us.

"You'll enjoy this," said Dad. "But if anyone asks who you are, try not to say much. Tell them you're our daughter-in-law. Very few Anglos have ever seen the dances and the ceremonies, and we like to keep it that way."

The car came to a halt above a huge valley, heavily wooded, mainly with pine trees, full of traditional tepees, set in circles and family groups. The smell of wood smoke wafted up from one area, where a huge amount of food was being prepared, and there were one or two large marquees set up in the centre. Flatbreads and chilli were being served to all who needed to eat, alongside the ubiquitous bottles of Coca-Cola.

We parked up, unloaded all the gear and made our own camp as the daylight faded. What hit me more than anything was the constant sound of the many drummers. The beat was hypnotic and unrelenting, and above it the sound of men and women singing chants which their ancestors had sung for thousands of years. This went on, hour after hour through the night, so I didn't really understand why we had brought sleeping bags. This wasn't an occasion for sleeping.

I don't remember exactly what I ate or drank in total, but the food was tasty. We all watched a large group of girls, all dressed in cream coloured buckskin, with moccasins on their feet dancing back and forth within the largest marquee. It was their initiation ceremony into puberty. Young men in another tent were performing similar dances.

The noise from the drumming, and the chanting was all

pervasive and eventually went deep inside one's bones. Music and dancing – it is said that rhythm is the first thing children in the womb understand and align with, and the very last thing someone with advanced dementia can recognise and respond to.

All through the night the festivities, the drumming, the dancing, the feasting continued. The febrile energy within the valley was diametrically opposite to the condescending myths of poor backward communities, full of drunks and low achievers, with which I had been regaled in the white communities of Southern California when I had asked about Native Americans.

These were people with a ten-thousand-year history, a spirituality which made that of the white settlers look naïve and shallow rooted, and a live, tragic story to tell. Through the power of those stories, their children were learning first-hand of their connection to the land which bore them.

As dawn flung its sharp sunlight up over the mid-summer skies, our family piled back into the car, and we set off once again through the pine forests to make the 100-mile trip home. We left at first light, but, to no-one's surprise, soon ran out of diesel and rolled into a tiny town where the one gas station was yet to open.

A short walk with a fuel can followed and we ended up in a traditional backwoods American diner where a woman in a dressing-gown cooked us sausage and pancakes, and an old arthritic cowboy came in demanding coffee with legs as bow-legged as a cartoon character. I remember feeling totally, ecstatically happy. It was the best July 4th weekend I ever spent, and I never wanted it to finish.

Mountain top experiences though, by their very nature,

don't last of course, so on the Monday I re-joined my bus, and fielded the questions about how my strange weekend with "The Indians" had gone. It had been really too intense to talk about, but when I mentioned in later years where I had been and what I had seen, especially to my Californian friends, few seemed really to believe me.

"We've never heard of anyone doing that," they said. "Nor anything like it."

Our partial cross-country trip finished with an experience of mid-west America, in a tiny town somewhere in North Kansas. I stayed with a Methodist family, in a white picket-fenced, painted wooden house, straight out of a Mark Twain novel.

My host lady told me why the town Council had volunteered to host a rumbustious bus load of foreign students.

"We felt we needed to do something to show we aren't really racist. We felt so ashamed last year. Our music society booked a pianist out of a catalogue to come to give a recital. Everyone was excited to meet this musician from New York, and there was a lot of competition to host him for the weekend.

"But when he got off the train, he was black! We had never had a black man come to our town before. No-one would put him up in their house. It was so shameful.

"In the end the minister housed him, and we tried to hide the fact that we were all so prejudiced. The concert went ahead. People attended, and it was lovely music. But after he left on the train on the Sunday afternoon to return to New York, the minister raised the issue in Church and made us confront some of our prejudices.

"You see, most folk here have never been west of the Colorado, or east of the Missouri. And many have never even been to Kansas City. They had never seen a black man in real life."

This was in 1971 and the people in that little Kansas town had admitted they were ignorant of their own country, let alone the world. I was very ignorant too, but I was beginning to learn something about both.

CHAPTER
4

Long skirts and gas meters
1971-1977 Cambridge, England

When I went back to England and found all the money had
changed, and the cars and houses seemed to have shrunk in
size by fifty percent since I'd left, I was determined to stay
as open to the world as possible. For the rest of the summer,
I took a job in a printing works making envelopes for the
NatWest bank.

It paid 20 pence an hour, or 30 cents, and I cut my fingers
to pieces on the paper cutter. We were supposed to make 250
envelopes an hour, a target which was impossible to meet,
given the blunt cutter, ancient work benches and inadequate
little glue pots. You earned sixpence bonus an hour if you
exceeded your target, but I never saw any of the women in the
section achieve this.

I stuck it out for six weeks. Some of the women working
at the same job had done it for thirteen years. It was a small
company with one canteen where we ate our lunches.

There were three tables. The directors' table had a white
cloth tablecloth and a cut-glass little vase of fresh flowers

and silver-plated cutlery. The foremen's table had a plastic tablecloth and a pot of plastic flowers, with steel knives and forks. The workers' table, where all of us were women, had no tablecloths, no flowers and cheap plastic cutlery.

But we all ate the same food, so that was the main thing. I thought it was rather funny, but no-one else seemed to share my sense of the absurdity of this class distinction.

I found my short work experience as an envelope maker both bizarre and amusing. It was a salutary experience and a very appropriate end to an astounding year in my education about how the world worked beyond the little town where I was born.

After my gap-year adventures in America, and my very short career as an envelope maker exploring the true tedium of being a "low-skilled" worker, I went up to Cambridge University and plunged into an exotic world of academia, student theatre, and another reality altogether.

Young people may not believe it today, but in my time, if you were accepted at a university, then your tuition fees were paid for you, and you were even given a maintenance grant which more than covered your accommodation and living costs. I went to study at Cambridge with virtually no money and emerged with no debts, despite never having to work part-time, except during the long summer vacations, when I earned money in order to travel. Getting into debt was virtually unheard of unless you went completely wild.

Government grants in those days, paid for all the University fees and accommodation costs. It was the golden era of British education, when excellent universities were opening their doors to more students from working class backgrounds, and giving them the chance to work for real degrees, in hard meaningful subjects.

It was also the era of the foundation of the Open University, of new centres, and new colleges. Under the Labour government of Harold Wilson, real and positive changes were enabled. So many of us were the first in our families to go to university, and we really valued the privilege so long denied to poorer people.

A few of my fellow students at Newnham College did obviously come from much wealthier families. They tended to have names like Griselda and Candace. Their fathers were largely ambassadors and professors, famous writers and scientists. Most of their mothers seemed less famous in general, but no-one it seemed had, like me, a dad who was a fireman and mum who had scraped her way out of secretarial work to become a teacher of the very youngest.

I often felt I was living in an Edwardian novel. Long skirts were the fashion then, and especially favoured, given the biting east winds we were all assured came straight off the steppes of Central Asia. We used to huddle round our tiny gas fires, wearing our coats and with fingerless mittens, trying to write essays on Spinoza, or Classical Greece, and in my case, the paintings of Raphael.

But my three years as an undergraduate were among the happiest in my life. I had a whole university library to read, good mates, who have remained so for life, and more music and drama than I had time to absorb. I also had more money than I had ever seen before. I carved out a place for myself upstairs in the University Library, and developed a routine for study which I learned from a man in our History cohort, who had just left the army.

Geoffrey told me how horrified he was by the careless attitude many of the undergraduates took towards turning up to lectures. He considered being given the chance to study the biggest privilege in the world, and was determined not to waste a moment of it. So, he was on campus by 9 o'clock sharp every weekday morning, and never left until 6pm.

"Don't fritter your time away," he said. "You'll regret it in later life if you do."

By my third year, when I was grappling with a new pathway to a degree through History of Art, I knew I had to follow Geoffrey's advice. But the subsequent absorption into books gave me the greatest pleasure, and it stilled my normally restless and easily distracted brain.

We stopped every morning though, at 11 am on the dot, when the smell of warm cheese scones percolated up through the airways from the Library cafeteria. I still have a fatal weakness for these, which was born then.

And Cambridge misogyny was beginning to creak its doors slowly open to the idea that women had the same rights to education as men. When I went up, there were exactly three undergraduate colleges which accepted female students, and, even then, the poor girls out at Girton College were four miles up a hill out of the town. That was a long and tiring ride on a bicycle, deliberately chosen to dissuade young men from visiting. At Newnham we were more accessible, and therefore more vulnerable.

Looking back, I later realised that I had had several "#metoo" experiences with "dates" who had physically accosted me, escorted me home to my college and then banged viciously on my door after paying a pound or two for a lasagne at the Eros restaurant. Drink and a sense of entitlement had turned them into monsters. They are now probably distinguished retired barristers, business directors, civil servants and clergymen.

England in 1971 was heading for recession. Power cuts, political enmity and strikes seemed to be the backcloth to my first year of University, but I buried myself in history books, student theatricals and the joys of cheap pasta.

I slept on a lumpy horsehair mattress in my renowned Cambridge women's college, and consoled myself that the holey curtains which failed to stop the rain coming through the casements were the same curtains which had been ineffectually drawn by generations of similarly earnest blue-stockings. I remember how my father was appalled at the ragged accommodation. I was enthralled. I could always wear two vests, and the library was magnificent.

I learned the tricks of student life. I still have a recipe called "Sue's 6 and a half pence fish pie". Everything you needed cost six and a half pence each in Sainsbury's, and it tasted damn good! There was also the Eros restaurant where you could order a small spaghetti, (obviously intended as a starter, but it still filled a stomach) for forty pence. The British currency had all been decimalised while I had been in America, so I was still fumbling through the new coinage months after everyone else.

We lived on our bicycles, flying through the streets to supervisions in our long skirts, long boots and long scarves. I had a boyfriend who was a Russian scholar and addicted to Chekhov plays so I was in three of them altogether, playing Irina in *Three Sisters*, and Olga in *Ivanov*. In those days I had a better bone structure and a bigger imagination, and slipped in and out of the present day into nineteenth-century Russia with surprising ease.

Some of my contemporaries went on to become politicians, one now wears blindingly awful colourful clothes and travels the world's railways for a living. A girl, just a little younger than I was, became Shadow Home Secretary. Others became household names through comedy and the wonderfully seductive world of television.

I never did embark on an illustrious career, but I had the privilege of living and enjoying Cambridge for three years longer than most of my friends by, (according to my mother), injudiciously marrying the chaplain from the college across the road, at the end of my third year.

At the end of my third "Michaelmas Term," I joined a University travelling drama group as wardrobe mistress on a tour round Europe as the aspiring thespians performed *Hamlet* in many different lovely venues, including Bruges, Heidelberg, Berne and Chambery. It was December, approaching Christmas. I especially remember the wonderful warm cafes in Heidelberg where you could play chess and listen to Baroque music while consuming 'Ghluwein' and other mulled drinks. The temperature was freezing, but the city was entrancing. We took the Philosopher's Walk, and felt very sophisticated.

We were hosted by very warm, generous people who must have been the European equivalents of members of the Rotary Club or something similar, and I recall staying in some very affluent and luxurious houses along the way. I remember being offered fillet steak and ice-cream, things which in three-day-week Britain I had almost forgotten existed.

We finally finished our theatre tour in Paris, two days before Christmas, and three of us were accidently left behind when the coach thought we were making our own way home (well, that was their excuse, but I certainly did not believe them). Somehow, we had to cross Paris, find a train at the Gare du Nord, and get ourselves to Calais in time to reconnect with the other thirty or so students on the bus before the ferry for Dover left.

The only trouble was, we had no money, or at least nowhere near enough. We pooled our pitiful resources. One of us had some Swiss Francs, another had a little British cash, so without much hope at all, we three lost sheep managed to get to the great station by public transport and presented ourselves at the ticket office.

It was two days before Christmas. The man behind the glass took pity on us, and gave us tickets in exchange for our collection of small change in various currencies. In short, we made it to Calais before the bus. In fact, we could see it drawing up as we sat in the gallery of the ferry terminal, and so we made it back home. I tore the organising people into tiny pieces of confetti though, when I met them again. I am little but I am quite fierce when sufficiently provoked, and they were duly chastened.

Between the academic years, in the summer of 1973, I worked as a student guide for American high school students in London, and the money I earned paid for a four-week trip round Turkey and Greece in late August and September.

I travelled with my first serious boyfriend, but there was a slight problem. We had already parted some months earlier, partly because he had presented me with a casserole dish for my twenty-first birthday present. (He has subsequently made a very successful, if unlikely, career teaching couples to have ecstatic tantric sex.)

It was awkward, but we were both too poor, and maybe too motivated to travel, to let it stop us making the trip. We co-existed as grumpy friends, but to the local people we met, innkeepers etc., we had to claim to be married, which worked, well, most of the time.

I still remember the Turkish for "married," something like "Evli." We travelled together because I wanted to look at ruins and he wanted to go to Asia, so Turkey was a compromise. We had little money and no firm plans. I took a *Teach Yourself Turkish* book, and my companion carried a war-weary copy of *Ulysses* he wanted to finish. In the event, he learned Turkish much better than I did, and I read the Joyce, cover to cover.

We embarked on a rickety old ship from Istanbul along the Black Sea coast as far as the Armenian border, and then crossed the mountains by local buses. The back of the bus often held half a dozen women, several with babies on their laps, who were all completely shrouded in what seemed to be heavy goat-hair blankets.

The buses were always crowded, with boys clinging to the roof rack and Turkish music loudly blaring out. They would leave at 4 am, 5 am or 6 am, each morning. If you took the 6 am bus, you were generally thought to be a complete sluggard, as the day was half over.

In the bus-stations, ferocious Turkish soldiers would be seen eating tiny bowls of rice-pudding together, or drinking the syrupy red tea with sixteen spoons of sugar, a brew which more than made up for the lack of mental stimulation of forbidden alcohol.

On these buses, the poorest, and the women were consigned to the back. Several of the female passengers were usually woefully travel-sick, and we could hear and smell them throwing up behind us, but none of them lifted their blankets, or asked the driver to stop. It all seemed grossly unfair, and the men down at the front appeared oblivious.

On one such bus-ride, we travelled on towards the Syrian border, and somewhere, I don't remember where, my friend and I decided we'd had enough, and asked to be set down. We found a tiny inn and left our rucksacks in the care of its owner, then decided to take a hike to a famous Islamic shrine a few miles away.

The sun grew hotter, and the road was very dusty. Everywhere seemed white and almost shimmering in the heat. Then ahead of us, we saw two small figures on the road.

They were walking the same way as us, but much more slowly, so we soon caught them up. One was an old woman, bent double under a sack of flour she had obviously walked to the town to buy, or have ground. But with her, was a small boy, probably a grandson, who was about eight to ten years old. He was dressed in something ragged and black, and had bare feet. They both looked as poor as mice.

In a casual, friendly way, my not-quite boyfriend offered to carry the woman's load for her, and she gratefully handed it over. He soon had to hand it on to me though, because we were both surprised how very heavy it was. We passed it back and forth between us, and so made progress for about two miles, as the road climbed higher up through the stony hillsides. It was a hard, hot walk.

Meanwhile the little boy took a fancy to me and I realised with great shock that he only had one eye, and his left hand hung uselessly down beside him. Some horrible accident must have befallen him, but we could not find out what exactly of course. Our strange meeting was held completely in silence.

The little boy kept looking at my clothes, in particular, a

lightweight blue jumper I had tied knotted round my waist. He plucked at it, obviously wanting it. I smiled but shook him off, and our little tug of war continued until we reached the shrine we wanted to visit.

"Please! Please! Give me your blue jumper!" he pleaded silently, gazing at me intently with his one eye.

"No, no! Don't ask me! It's my favourite jumper. It's my only sweater on this trip!" I silently shouted back at him.

He looked very close to tears, but my heart hardened, and of course I won. We gave them a few pennies in consolation, and they walked on, the grandmother once again shouldering her load, and the little boy looking back at me.

As soon as they had gone, of course I immediately felt horrible. I could have easily given him the blue jumper, which I could replace for three dollars in any market. I ran back down to the road, and looked forwards, and then back. It ran long and straight through the hills, but nowhere, nowhere were an old lady and her little grandson walking. The road was empty, for miles, in both directions.

There is a sad little postscript to this story. I kept the blue jumper, but a month later, in a youth hostel in Athens, I was packing to go home, and couldn't fit all my souvenirs into my rucksack. I looked for something to jettison, and my gaze fell on the old blue jumper. Without thinking I pulled it out and tossed it into the waste bin.

Only then did the face of that little boy come back to me, as clear as day. I had met with an angel, a messenger of truth and love, but I hadn't listened. I still think of him, and wonder where he is today, if he is still alive.

From the white Kurdish highlands beyond Diyarbakir, our journey then took us, all the time by local buses, to the city of Adana, the modern equivalent of Tarsus, in the far south east of Turkey. There we had a very bizarre visit to a friend I had made in California, a charming and very friendly girl who had been on the same exchange programme and who had lived with a family in the same city as me, attending a different but neighbouring high school.

I had written to Meryl to say I was coming to Turkey and asking if it would be possible to meet. She was now back home, studying at her local university, but was enthusiastic, and said her "fiancé" would meet us when we arrived in Istanbul, and help us book tickets for the Black Sea boat trip.

This had all gone well. Said was a really friendly guy, who helped us negotiate the chaotic ticket offices in the Istanbul port area, and showed us all around the city, including the Santa Sophia Mosque, formerly the magnificent Byzantine cathedral, with its shining blue mosaics, and gigantic censor.

When we parted, he said, "I look forward to seeing you when I get home to Adana. Could you just do me one favour? Can you introduce me to my fiancée and her family? Our relationship is actually secret and her parents have never met me. If you introduce me as a friend of yours, then I can start negotiating with her father to come to visit."

I had never heard of such a strange necessity, but when we met up with my friend Meryl, I realised her life back home in Turkey was quite different from the freedoms she had enjoyed in California. To start with, when we called her from the bus-station to say we had arrived, she could not even leave the house to meet us, but asked us to get a taxi.

She attended college, but was expected to be home immediately when classes finished, and for the rest of the time was virtually confined to quarters. Her father, who seemed to sit around all day in pyjamas, was deeply suspicious, but spoke no English, so we could talk quietly as she struggled to explain just how difficult it had been to adjust to life back in conservative Adana, and how impossible it had proved to be open with her family. She had a younger brother though, who understood a little English, and he was equally suspicious and condescending towards his older sister.

We went through the charade of talking to Meryl about this really nice guy we had met in Istanbul, who just happened to hail from the same town as her. While we were visiting, could we call him and invite him over while we were staying with Meryl and her family? She translated this fairy tale to her parents.

They agreed, and she organised the phone call. Said came over pretty quickly, driving his father's Mercedes, and while studiously ignoring Meryl, paid his compliments to her father and mother, and treated us like long lost friends. He offered to take their whole family out on a day trip, and as they had no car, this was irresistible, so we all climbed aboard, and set off up to some local shrine.

It was a good day, and at the end Said, who was no fool, manage to neutralise Meryl's brother's opposition and suspicions by offering to show him his motorbike, and maybe take him for a ride on it.

When we left the following morning, Meryl waved us away at her front gate, and thanked us for our help. It was now all going to be fine, she assured us. Said would introduce his (wealthy) parents to hers, and then they could move forward to a formal engagement.

I do hope it worked out, because I never heard from either

of them again, but maybe our turning up in their lives had made a difference. I really hope so.

Our month in Turkey was also memorable because of the unpleasant fact that I nearly died, or so it seemed at the time. I had unwisely eaten an orange ice-lolly, bought from a stall on the street in Antalya several days later, and within a couple of hours on the next bus ride, knew I was going to be most unwell.

I ended up spending more than a week in a tiny hotel, running a very high fever, and throwing up constantly until the hotel owner, who nursed me tenderly and hated my boyfriend as a negligent husband, demanded I go to hospital as he didn't want me dying in his inn. Turkey only had squat toilets in those days, but I won't dwell on those unnecessarily unpleasant details.

The only book I had with me was the aforementioned *Ulysses* and I had already read it cover to cover, the long hours of misery also punctuated by the regular, and raucous electronic calls to prayer from a neighbouring minaret. It was surreal to say the least. My pretend husband had to endure the reproachful company of our landlord, who once took him out to a breakfast of sheep's eyeball soup, a punishment, I'm sure.

I really didn't want to go into a Turkish hospital. Memories of the Crimean war filled my fevered imagination, but Fethye, where we were at the time, was a quiet village, with a very pleasant, clean small hospital, and the doctor in charge was actually an Ankara-based physician who had a summer house on the south coast, and was acting as a holiday locum.

When I was dragged inside the hospital by my two male companions, the Ex. and Mr Grumpy, the Doctor took one look at my bright green tongue, and said. "Para-typhoid."

Well, no-one had told me! I'd had shots against typhoid, but not this ersatz version, it seemed. They kindly admitted me free of charge, and put me on a course of the right antibiotics, along with a very boring but effective diet of boiled white rice, and boiled white potatoes, without salt.

I shared a room with an old man on the same diet, not at all what I expected from such a Muslim society. He was not a great conversationalist, so life was very boring, but I began to feel some hope I would not die there. I finished *Ulysses*. The doctor's daughter, a pretty girl of about eighteen, who wanted to practise her English, visited me with tales of life beyond my little ward. Where my travelling companion had gone to, I had no idea.

Then on my fourth day in hospital he burst through the door and shouted, "Come on! We have to leave!"

"Not possible," I said. "I can barely stand, let alone make it to the bus-station."

"No choice," he replied. "Greece and Turkey have declared war, and there is just one more sailing out of here, from Marmaris, to evacuate the foreigners, then there will be a complete embargo. We may never get another sailing, and as you know we have no money left."

It was true. We had about £20 between us, so couldn't settle in Turkey for the next few years.

Somehow, I crawled into my clothes and discharged myself, much to the doctor's displeasure, but he gave me another week's supply of the antibiotics and told me to try to stick to boiled water or bottled Coca-Cola until I returned to the UK.

I was rather surprised how loose fitting all my garments seemed, but as I hadn't looked in a mirror, I didn't really understand how thin I looked. My friend kindly carried my rucksack along with his own, and we made it onto the next bus, and by a small miracle onto the last boat out of Turkey some hours later.

We had other adventures, including sleeping on cots in an outside courtyard, in an inn in Crete where the landlord's wife stabbed him in the stomach overnight. Everyone else had endured a sleepless night, but I slept on my cot like a baby. I had somehow managed to drink most of a bottle of banana brandy and passed out for ten hours straight.

But this novel method of recovery did seem to cure my para-typhoid and renewed my strength. When I reached home a week or so later, I couldn't understand why my mother screamed when she saw me, but then I had cleverly managed to lose thirty pounds weight in as many days.

CHAPTER

5

Moving on
1977-1983 The "Third Sector"

At the end of my third year of university I married the Chaplain of the neighbouring college to ours at Cambridge. My drama club friends all fell about laughing when I announced my engagement, and I realised that maybe I should have thought this through a bit more. He had beguiled me with his lovely speaking voice and his red Morgan Sports car. But even though the car was sold almost immediately, for the sake of my fiancé's Springer Spaniel puppy, and I discovered I would for ever be landed with a "vicar's wife" tag, we have not quite yet had sufficient time to repent of our speedy romance over the last forty-six years.

We spent three more years in Cambridge, during which time I decided to drop out of a post-grad diploma course in history teaching.

"But you won't be able to be a history teacher!" scolded my mother.

Precisely. One month on teaching practice had made me very cynical and unwilling to return so soon to the school life

I had only just escaped. I listened to the teachers talking in the staff room.

"Well, I wouldn't send my kids to this dump," said one, who was supposed to be my mentor in the Cambridgeshire village college where I was attached. I caught flu, and reconsidered my options. I then resigned by letter, and looked for other work.

I found it, as an area schools' fundraiser for Help the Aged, then a novel charity still in its infancy. The office for our team was notionally in New Bond Street, London, but mostly we worked from home and lived in our cars. In London, the charity was effectively squatting in a hairdressing salon, with boards placed over a row of washbasins instead of desks, and swivel chairs leftover from the previous tenants' need to shampoo the backs of their customers' heads. It was crazily managed and under resourced, and I really liked it, to begin with.

My patch started as East Anglia and several more counties in rural south-east England, but soon extended from Sheffield down to Oxford and into Outer London, Watford to Woodford. I would get up at 5 am in Cambridge and drive through the curling mists to Eltham in South London to take a morning assembly. But I enjoyed the travel, and the fun of meeting a colleague near Bedford in a transport café, eating giant wedges of bacon butties and drinking mugs of tea. I soon managed to upgrade to the role of training officer, and had an even more unwieldy patch. I virtually lived on the road.

My car was a Ford Escort, but my trainees, poor things, had baby Fiats ("Fix it again tomorrow" was a realistic nickname in those days). Once in Leicester, as she met me at the station and drove me to her flat, one brand new recruit tried to change gear and the entire gear stick and associated gubbins came off in her hand. We looked together at a hole in the base of the car, as the road continued to disappear under us.

She had been a British Airways air-stewardess, and had high standards of speech and decorum, but even she swore as we narrowly avoided death. As I remember, her father wrote her resignation letter for her the same week.

I lived this crazy life for nearly three years, but then, early in 1977 gave up fundraising for Help the Aged, in order to give birth to my elder son, Chris, who has followed me in one huge regard. He loves to travel, and has made friends all over the world. In recent years we worked together as development consultants and on some of the trips I write about here, he was an invaluable support.

With a brand-new baby, a Citroen Dyane, two large dogs, and a ginger cat, we decided to leave Cambridge and head for the hills. My husband took a post with the Diocese of Carlisle so we moved to the head of Ullswater, under the magnificent group of fells round Helvellyn. Here for close to three years, my world shrank to the mountains I could see around me, but rarely climbed, as I was either pregnant or breast-feeding.

One day in early spring when the snowdrops were beginning to peep through the snow, my little boy asked me what the "yellow sticky stuff" was on his face.

"It's sunshine, darling. I know it feels strange." We had just endured our second Cumbrian winter and Vitamin D was in very short supply.

When there was a knock on the front door, I was pleased by the distraction as I was trying to take towelling nappies off the washing line which were completely stiff like frozen cardboard.

Our visitor was the Area Secretary for Christian Aid, with a patch to cover from Manchester out to the Isle of Man. Barbara was the sort of woman I could relate to, with a car-boot full of promotional literature and a fearless attitude. She asked if we could find someone to organise a local fund-raising committee for Christian Aid Week in three months' time. I was easily persuaded, and after vowing never to work for a charity again, I found myself drawn in, this time to a whole world of need and projects for development. After we left Cumbria and moved south to be nearer our parents, I waited until my younger son, Tim, started school, and then looked for work in the voluntary sector.

I ended up doing very similar work to Barbara's, as Area Secretary across Cheshire and South Manchester. My main task, in order to sustain the work of over a hundred local committees and single activists, was to tell stories, to personalise the work we were doing, and this was to prove all too easy. There was so much to share.

I spent fourteen years altogether with Christian Aid, managing the North West team of Area Staff and becoming active in several national campaigns and educational initiatives. They were fulfilling years, but demanding, as most of the meetings I attended were in the evening, and I shared child-care responsibilities with a very busy partner.

On leaving Cheshire in 1996 my husband's church work took us to Derbyshire, where I found work as an A level politics teacher in a Jesuit boarding school. My attempts to thwart my mother's ambitions for me to become a teacher were not altogether successful, and I also moved from there a few years later to taking up a post as tutor in a Methodist College. This in its turn took me back to Africa in 2002, and from then on, I devoted myself to working for marginalised communities round the world.

PART
TWO

CHAPTER

6

The Philippines
1984

My first serious trip was to the Philippines in 1984, where I discovered what there was to learn at the back of buses, or Jeepneys as they are universally known there. It was through Christian Aid that I went to the Philippines, the first time I thought my children were old enough to stay with their dad and my mother looking after them for three weeks. I mainly travelled alone, because my colleague's itinerary was slightly different, and I remember the Cathay Pacific jet taking us right over the remote western bamboo forests of China.

I imagined the pandas chewing their way patiently through their low protein diet somewhere in the hills below, and embraced the wild thought of how very small the world is, when you looked at it from above (the international space station can now circle it in 90 minutes!).

The Philippines form a beautiful archipelago of more than 7600 islands in the western Pacific Ocean. Arriving in Manila, the first thing to notice is the suffocating heat, which hits you as soon as the plane door opens. It is like walking through a sauna on full power. I was met, and cordially escorted to a vehicle and then we set off through the appalling reality which is any major city close to the equator.

Mile after mile of "informal" housing stretched in each direction, suburbs, but not as the people living in Los Angeles might know them. There were long unpaved alleyways crowded with tiny stores, screaming taxis, cars, and squadrons of Mercedes limousines pushing through as if they owned the place, which of course they did.

So many dwellings were made of little more than cardboard and corrugated tin, and everywhere the sound boomed out of street traders calling, most of whom seemed only of school age. Children stopped us at every traffic light, selling gum, yesterday's newspapers, tiny packets of paper tissues, little bags of water. They ran in and out of the traffic like sparrows. Tiny, ragged sparrows.

I was conveyed, eventually, to a thoroughly respectable and functional church hostel, and waited for my colleague to join me. Our trips round Manila over the next few days showed us so much more of people's real lives. We visited rubbish dumps, home to 100,000 people, political prisons, and wretched industrial work camps where we met the textile workers producing high end ski-wear for the European market.

What can I say? Over the years I have become hardened, I suppose, to human suffering, but recalling that first visit to the Philippines brings back in technicolour the painful stories shared with me, and which I witnessed first-hand.

An endnote, before I begin. On my final day in the Philippines, while I waited for my flight back to Hong Kong to visit Vietnamese refugees in detention centres, a well-dressed, kindly-spoken affluent fellow passenger in the airport asked me how I had enjoyed my visit, and where I had gone in her beautiful country. I named a few destinations, and the time I had spent in various notorious slums and prisons.

"My poor young woman," she said, "What a shame you were so badly advised. I wish you had come to stay with me. I would have given you a much nicer time on your holidays!"

The Philippines, like so many hard-pressed southern nations, has to accommodate itself to the demands of multi-national companies by creating free-trade zones, where national minimum wages, and health and safety protocols don't apply, and where taxes and other annoyances are minimal. We went to a large factory, just outside Manila, to hear the stories of young women working in the textile industry.

We met with them in a small room hired by the Young Christian Workers, a struggling support agency for them, which was generally side-lined by the mainstream churches, and actively discouraged by the government. The girls were all between fifteen and twenty-one.

"We have one bunk between three of us, as we only need it for a third of a 24-hour day. We are usually working the rest of the time. We sew ski jackets, like these." They showed me some. They looked familiar and I recognised the brand-name labels inside. They were selling for £50 to £60 each at the time in our local department stores in the UK.

"All the material, zippers, buttons, threads, are shipped in from elsewhere, Vietnam or India, wherever they can be bought most cheaply. We do the sewing, as the Filipina girls are the best sewers, and the cheapest in the world.

"We start at age fifteen and we are usually classed as apprentices until we are eighteen. That means they can pay us even less"

"How much?"

"Maybe five dollars a week, but we get pay docked for all sorts of reasons. If we go to the comfort room too much, if we are late at the machine by even a minute or two." The comfort rooms in the Philippines are usually latrine toilets, some of the most uncomfortable places in the world.

"The place isn't well lit, and we often get sick. We are very often made to work far into the night to complete orders. Girls here normally don't survive long after they turn twenty. They get lung disease, or bad backs. Their eyesight goes or they simply give up from exhaustion. Then the company lets them go. There are always more young girls waiting for jobs."

Then they asked us, "Can you tell us how much these clothes are sold for in Europe and the USA? We're always told our wages are so low because people can't afford to buy them if they were higher."

We told them, soberly, that each padded jacket would easily fetch $100 dollars in our shops. The room went silent, as the shocked expressions on the girls' faces told the story. Then almost inaudibly, we could hear sobbing, as they realised just how calculatedly their employers had exploited their labour, and destroyed their health and their youth.

There is a small twist to this tale. Months later, the local fundraising committee for my charity back home in Cheshire was running a coffee morning to raise funds, some of which might be sent to the Christian Young Workers of Manila. The committee told me, "Such good news, our local clothing company, Baird Textiles, have sent through five of their new range ski jackets for us to sell at our event. So generous of them, don't you think?" I looked in the jackets for their country of origin. Yes, you guessed it. The labels all said, "Made in the Philippines".

The trip continued. By now we were a long way south of Manila, on the island of Mindanao, and we had been travelling now for more than a hundred kilometres. Night had fallen long ago.

The old jeep lurched and ground its way through the jungle on unmade tracks, and our friend Romy, who was driving, had to peer into the seemingly impassable undergrowth to navigate us through. We never went faster than ten miles an hour, but then finally, sometime after 9 pm he put his feet down on the clutch and we rolled to a standstill.

"Are we there?" we asked. It seemed to be in the middle of nowhere.

"No, not exactly," he smiled.

"Damulog is another two hours away, but I think it would be safer to stay here for the night. You see, the brakes failed twenty miles back, but I couldn't stop there, it would have been too dangerous, so I have nursed us along in first gear. But here, this is a good place. I have friends near here who will put us up for the night. Just wait for a few minutes."

And he disappeared into the black night.

When he returned, it was with a smiling, shy man, with very work-worn hands.

"Welcome, welcome! You are most welcome!"

We watched as all our bags, and the essential equipment carried on any Filipino journey was unloaded, and we were escorted through the darkness by torchlight. As we stumbled out from the trees, we saw that there was one very small house in a clearing. Built of bamboo, it seemed to have one room about twelve feet squared, with little bamboo steps up to the door, and judging from the snuffling and grunting noises, a load of animals kept under the floor in a sort of ground level stable.

A woman came forward and grasped our hands. She spoke little or no English, but she bade us welcome. In the light of the torch we could see the entire floor was covered with the thin straw woven sleeping mats, on which lay, packed like sardines, a large number of small children. There was no room, at all, for anyone else.

"No, no," we protested, as she invited us in. "You are obviously full up. We can sleep in the vehicle."

Our friend interpreted what she said next. "Children, children, how can you be so selfish? Move onto your sides, and make room for our visitors to sleep!"

Each little child obediently turned onto his or her side, and squashed up against his neighbour. By some magic, this created just enough space for two large women.

My colleague decided to undress into her pyjamas, which were white, and capacious. Then she needed to answer the call of nature. It was irresistible. Fourteen pairs of eyes, including mine, watched as she bravely walked to the end of the clearing with her bobbing torch and went behind the trees at the end. Then we all solemnly watched the large ghostly white figure come back. We all shut our eyes as she mounted the steps, and pretended we had not watched her expedition. What I did do in the toilet department I can't remember, but I wasn't going to provide another floor show.

I turned on my side, like a good neighbour and found my face pressed close up against a sleeping four-year-old. So, we all settled down, for the night. Which, as it turned out, wasn't long! Before 4 am, a great buzz of noise came up through the single layer floor of bamboo poles on which we slept. All the chicks, hens, the piglet, a puppy, tiny goat and of course several cockerels began to chunter to themselves and to each other from inside their makeshift accommodation under the house stilts. These woke the children, and when one or two woke, then all of us followed suit. It seemed rather rude to try to stay lying down on the sleeping mat, as we took up at least a third of the house.

Their mother was up as the dawn gradually spread up the sky from the east. The children went outside to wash at the pump, and dress in their school clothes, then they came in and the older ones all received a small ball of cold cooked white rice, wrapped in a banana leaf parcel. It would be their breakfast and lunch combined.

It seemed early to leave for school, I commented to our friend, who was acting as translator. "Oh, they have a long way to walk to school. It takes forty-five minutes each way."

Wanting to make a small gesture of thanks, I produced a ball-point pen from my bag and offered it to the oldest daughter, a girl of maybe twelve years old.

She immediately handed it to her mother with undoubted excitement. "Mama, Mama, look! We have a pen now."

"Give it to me I will put it on our little hanging shelf, see! It will be so useful when we need to sign a document or fill in a form."

The pen was obviously far too precious, just to be given to a child to take to school. I thought of my own children's pencil cases, bulging with all sorts of pens and coloured markers. I was sure my sons had no idea how many they had. One pen. But a powerful tool. The gift of writing, of education, which those children were walking so far through the jungle to attain, even now the memory of that one pen reminds me of what a privilege it is.

Within an hour or two of the dawn, our friend and his mates had replaced the brake cable and we were on the road again. I never knew the names of our hosts that night, but their generosity, giving from the nothing they had, was spectacular. I have never forgotten them, or their children who slept sideways so I could sleep as well, and the joy over one pen.

People in the Philippines eat communally. Food is placed in the centre of the circle, or on the table, and whoever is present is automatically invited to eat. Hungry people will turn up close to a mealtime, and are rarely excluded. In this way, I saw daily re-enactments of the loaves and fishes' story from the Bible.

One great method I saw of stretching an egg round six people, was to slice an eggplant or aubergine vertically into strips, and then dip each slice into a beaten egg, diluted with a little water. These were then fried into a kind of fritter. Vital protein in an otherwise carbohydrate-heavy subsistence diet.

But sometimes the foreigner can get things very badly wrong. If you eat with others, then you are expected to share. My host, a British woman who had gone to the Philippines as a VSO volunteer for two years and stayed thirteen more, told me of one such gaffe, which stayed in people's minds as truly shocking for years after.

She and her husband had hosted a couple of young men, Europeans or North Americans, it didn't really matter from where. But these guys were just visiting, and had become really hungry. They were big fellows, with large appetites, and looking at the rice being prepared, one of them knew it wouldn't be enough for him, especially if it had to stretch round eight other people. So, he thought he would lend a hand by nipping off to the local Sari-Sari store and buying something to supplement the meal.

He came back with a tin of sardines. Everyone sat and was served with a small bowl of rice. People looked with some anticipation at the sardine tin. But the guy who had bought it simply opened it, and poured the entire contents over his one helping of rice. It was only a small tin of sardines after all, far too small to share.

What he hadn't realised, my friend explained, was that this was breaking the most fundamental rule of being either a host or a guest. You always share what you have.

If he had passed round his little tin, each person would have taken out a teaspoonful, and there would have been enough to savour the otherwise plain rice for everyone. The meal would have been made tasty, and the bonds of friendship strengthened.

As it was, a shocked silence fell over the company, and I am sure the poor visitor had no idea how he had caused such offence. But hopefully, by the end of his visit to the Philippines, he would have understood. It is impossible to spend any time with these gracious people and not do so.

The Archbishops and Bishops, some of whom were definitely from families connected with President Marcos, the then notorious ruler of the Philippines, and other leaders in the Army, lived in absolute palaces and rarely challenged the status quo. But there were some outstanding exceptions.

We visited one Catholic sister, who came from a wealthy family, and therefore had access to some private funds, with which she purchased a little house in the slums, overlooking an open sewer at the end of a filthy alleyway. There she ran a centre for the local poor, and also managed to lure the ordinands, who were studying for the priesthood in the regional seminary, to come to stay for a few weeks at a time as part of their training.

For many of these young men it was a devastating revelation. We met with a couple of trainee priests who said they had never known that poverty like this existed in their own country. They had been blind to it, even though they had chosen the priesthood as their vocation and had lived there all their life.

This inability to connect with people who do not share our privileges and blessings is a global phenomenon, and one which has troubled me all my life. It seems to be some sort of "selfish gene," which can infect whole societies, and can eventually lead to ethnic cleansing and mass atrocities. But it can also be cured, through education, yes, but, more powerfully, by a personal encounter with people who live on the edge, and really entering into their stories.

For these ordinands, their time in the little house had been truly life-changing, and one of the most valuable lessons in their training, just as my day in Tijuana had been for me.

At the end of the alley, ran a boulevard which actually led up to the local Archbishop's palace.

"Has he ever visited?" we asked the Sister in charge.

"Oh no, not yet," she laughed. "But I did see his limousine slow down to a crawl one day, as he drove past. I think I may be able to encourage him to stop, and walk down with me to see our little house before too long."

From Mindanao, I flew many miles north to Baguio, President Marcos's much publicised summer capital. It is a "resort" city higher up in the hills of Northern Luzon, and therefore a place of retreat from the heat of Manila. My friend Romy, who had been a Jesuit priest, said the pleasant retreat centre run by his order up there, had actually been a factor in his deciding to leave the priesthood.

Romy said he became a Jesuit and went through the many years' training, in order to be closer to the poor people, not remove himself from their struggles. The idea of decamping to the hills when the weather became uncomfortable, left him very uncomfortable indeed.

I had come to Baguio to take part in Tribal Filipino week. It was sponsored by the churches as a forum for the indigenous peoples' cultures and as publicity for their sufferings. Outside my hotel window were lilies, hibiscus flowers and gladioli. Their scent was addictive and above, the sky was a clear, cool blue, such a pleasant contrast from the steaming jungles of Mindanao.

At home it would be autumn, with thoughts turning towards Christmas and winter boots, mufflers against the cold, but here it was another world. I watched and observed the children who worked the streets beyond the hotel garden.

The first was a little cigarette boy who stood at the crossing, not ten feet away from me. He was seven, maybe eight, dressed in a ragged T-shirt and shorts. He carried a tray of American cigarettes and a few packets of sweets.

When the lights changed to red and the traffic halted in a haze of exhaust fumes he would dash out into the middle of the road and run back and forth between the cars. If he was very lucky a driver might occasionally lean out of his car window and buy a pack of cigarettes. For every pack he sold he made 25 centavos profit – one English penny – but he mainly sold cigarettes one at a time. The cigarette boy was there all day. His mother sold oranges further down the road and his baby sister sat in the dirt beside her on a ragged blanket. She never cried, but just sat in the exhaust fumes all day, silently.

In Baguio I also met Virginia, a young woman who spoke at the tribal peoples' conference. She worked in a strawberry and cut-flower plantation run by multi-national businessmen a few miles from the city. These are her own words which I recorded at the time.

"The work is hard physical labour and also skilled. We are all women and are paid 30 pesos a day (£1.20). For this we have to work eight hours without any break for rest or lunch. To get to our place of work high in the terraces we have to climb for four kilometres from the plantation gate, but we get no pay for the time it takes to walk that distance. Even if we run it takes at least 30 minutes. At harvest time we are made to work overtime, sometimes until 2 am. Most of us are mothers with young children so we get very anxious for our little ones at home. I ask you, what can we do?"

Virginia earned less than half the amount needed to even feed a family in the Philippines at that time. The strawberries and flowers she grew was on land forcibly taken from tribal people and sold abroad for a large profit. Armed guards stood at the gate of her place of work.

I saw another armed guard, this time besides a gigantic concrete statue of President Marcos's head. It had been carved into the mountainside overlooking some of the most beautiful landscapes in Asia, a grotesque pastiche of Mount Rushmore in the USA. The guards lived in a dilapidated shack, covered with painted crosses to ward off the spirits of the men killed during the statue's erection. Built between 1978 and 1981 it rose to 90 feet and looked out over a little used golf-course and a high-priced hotel complex.

The Ibaloi rice farmers who had held the land by ancestral rights for thousands of years had been evicted and even their pitiful compensation had been corruptly mismanaged. The statue reminded me of Shelley's poem "Ozymandias" which describes the demolished statue of a long dead King, and symbolised perfectly the vain glory and pomposity of a man whose face looks out over an empty land.

I was told that around 1978, the bust's construction had begun alongside the Marcos Highway, which was later officially renamed Aspiras-Palispis Highway. The bust was constructed by the Philippine Tourism Authority, under the orders of the President himself, and was meant to be the centre-piece of Marcos Park, something else Marcos named after himself.

After the People Power Revolution of 1986, the Ibaloi peoples slaughtered a pig and water buffalo and poured the animals' blood onto the bust to "exorcise" it and later filed a case to reclaim their land. The bust was bombed in 1989 by leftist rebels and sustained cracks and other minor damage.

Finally, the bust was completely destroyed using dynamite before dawn on December 29, 2002 by suspected treasure hunters. But it contained nothing. It has never been rebuilt.

It was while I was in Baguio that I met Gina, and started a friendship which was to last many years. She was a young woman of maybe twenty-three years old, and, when we met, she was standing in line in the hope of seeing some medical students who had arrived from the university and were offering a clinic for the poor. The queue was very long, and in the end, it wasn't trainee doctors at the end of it, but trainee dentists, which was very discouraging for all the parents of sick children hoping for help, and vaccinations.

Gina and I started to talk. Her English was good, and she introduced herself, her little boy who was maybe three years old, and his baby sister. Gina's first husband had died, and her second had proved so violent when she became pregnant, she had run away from him. "I called my baby girl, 'Joy,' because we were no longer in danger," she said.

"How do you support yourself and your children?" I asked.

"I collect empty Coca-Cola bottles from the back of bars and hotels or from the trash cans. Sometimes I have to pay a cent or two for them. Then I put them in a crate, and when I have three or more crates I put them on my head and carry them up to the bottling plant, and receive some more cents for them."

"How far is the bottling plant from where you collect the bottles?"

"Two and a half miles each way."

"And what about the children?"

"I carry Joy on my back, and Demi walks with me."

"How often do you do this?"

"About five times a day. If I do that I can earn enough, maybe two US dollars, to buy enough food, and pay rent and fuel for the day."

"You must get very tired."

"Yes, but when Demi is four, it will be better. Then I can leave Joy with him and I can work faster."

"Surely you mean when he is fourteen?"

"Oh, no, when he is four, he will be responsible enough to care for his sister. I will have weaned her by then and he can feed her rice water until I get home."

I was completely silenced by this.

Eventually the not-quite medical facility closed for a long lunch break, and Gina was still forty or so people from the front of the line. She hitched little Joy further up her back, and said, "I can't wait any longer. I don't think they will re-open today. Could I have your address? I would like to write to you."

"Sure, and give me yours."

We exchanged addresses, on a sheet of note paper I had torn from my book, and then started a friendship which lasted for more than ten years. I watched her walk away up the rough path from the local hall where the medical students had come, back to the marathon trudge around the city which was her daily work. Little Demi, three years old, went with her.

I stayed in correspondence with Gina for the next decade, and received letters from her all the time she struggled to make a living, first in Baguio, and then, against my advice, as a maid in Singapore and then in Hong Kong. I certainly helped her financially now and then, and assisted in getting a certificate in typing, for example, but in those years she never managed to escape the poverty trap. Keeping her kids fed, clothed, and then in school consumed her whole life.

Her sufferings and frustrations were huge, but her optimism remained. Our unequal friendship will make another book one day, as I have saved all her letters to me. In the course of my life, married to a Church of England clergyman, I moved many times, and at some stage we lost touch. I hope her life eventually gave her something back for the back-breaking labour of her twenties and thirties. She certainly inspired me.

The Churches I encountered in the Philippines were a strange paradox. It was 1984, and all the billboards for the

Catholic Church urged people to celebrate the birthday of the Virgin Mary. This was largely a fundraising exercise as people were cajoled into giving her birthday presents of cash. It had been figured by some PR genius, that as Mary was probably only a kid of fourteen when Jesus was born, then this year could be counted as her 2000th birthday. It was a good moneymaking scheme.

As for the Protestants, when the Americans gained the Philippines from Spain in a treaty of 1898 (during the ensuing war from 1898 to 1902, at least 200,000 civilians died, and some put the figure as high as a million), the accompanying Protestant churches decided to divide the islands up between them. This meant that if you were a Protestant and came from, for example, Mindanao then it was highly likely you would be a Congregationalist. If you came from northern Luzon, then the Methodists would be running the churches. The Baptists took over all the missionary work in the Western Visayas.

This seemed to me to be religious colonialism of the most blatant kind. However, only about 11% of Filipinos joined the Protestant churches following the earlier Spanish invasions. Catholicism held sway, and was obviously one reason why families were so huge.

I saw this when I visited a gold mining camp where the people lived in the most abject poverty in one-roomed housing, with no bathrooms. The whole community of workers had to use latrines and dirty facilities at the end of the street.

Many women I spoke to had upwards of ten children, and when they discovered I had two sons, they commiserated with me. "You poor soul! Sister, we will pray for you that the Lord will grant you many more children."

I begged them not to, saying I was very happy with two, but they weren't having any of it. I am so grateful that was one set of prayers which were never answered.

I remember a small local store had books to borrow on a stand, and they were all Mills and Boon romances. A yearning for romantic love obviously remained for these women whose husbands and children worked in the huge, desperately dangerous gold mines. The mines degraded all the surrounding hillsides and destroyed the forests which held the fragile eco-structure together. Landslides were very common as the watersheds disappeared.

CHAPTER

7

Prisons within Prisons
1984 Manila

Throughout our time in the Philippines we met many men and women, church workers, and community development leaders, who had been swept up because of the perceived threat they posed to the power of President Marcos. At that time, the harsh authority of that man's illegal regime pervaded the whole country with a sullen menace.

There was a hugely vulgar, massive statue to him on one of the main roads near Manila, and the armed police and military were everywhere. Armed militias were murdering community leaders.

I spoke to one priest who told me he had just identified the body of a local boy shot in the back and flung into a drainage ditch. The putrefaction in the 35-degree heat had been extreme, and had made him physically ill for days after.

While we were in Manila, we wanted to visit the prisoners of conscience who had been incarcerated, often without trial, by the regime. Our charity supported their cause, and especially the families often left without a breadwinner for months or years on end. Moreover, people in prison in the Philippines always needed family support to survive. Without supporters bringing them food they could literally starve on the totally inadequate rations.

Of all the prisoners in the large central prison in Manila, the political prisoners were the most harshly treated and the least accessible, so it took days of applications and arguing before we were given permission to visit. We went to two locations, the first was a prison within a prison. We went through gate after gate, into locked compounds through several internal checkpoints, finally to arrive in a very crowded covered yard about the size of a tennis court. This was the section of the prison housing the political prisoners. Overcrowded cells opened on to it all around. The air was fetid and the temperatures stifling.

Within this horrible prison in Manila, I met some of the saintliest people I have ever seen. One was a young woman, a church activist, who had her one-year-old child with her. The walls of her cell were so wet, she had planted vegetables in tin cans and hung them from nails in the concrete.

"They get watered automatically by the water running down the wall," she laughed. Her child had been born in that cell, and by some human miracle of cooperation between prisoners and their supporters, the child had not died, but thrived as her mother fed her. "I believe in God," she said, "because only through a miracle could my daughter have survived, and now she can even tolerate the prison food. We all cook together, whatever we have. We share everything."

Many of the prisoners, and there were far more men than women, passed their time by creating beautiful pictures of Filipino life from tiny slithers of bamboo. These were truly lovely and we bought several as "souvenirs" of our time in the country. By creating these, and other artwork the prisoners tried to help themselves and their families.

But getting any hope of release needed many hours of preparing legal appeals and trying to get due process, and the number of lawyers who were prepared to work pro bono was very low. It was also highly dangerous to be seen to be defending political prisoners, and they had their own families to consider.

One example of the crazy cruelty of the system was the man who had been in prison for one of the longest sentences. He had been a printer by profession, a quiet man, not an activist or an opposition politician. His local Catholic parish priest had asked him to print the parish magazine, a task he undertook every month.

But in this particular edition, the Church had advertised a public meeting. Everyone who attended that meeting had been arrested, beaten up or thrown into jail, including the priest. The printer, too, had been arrested, and given the longest prison sentence of all, for he had advertised the meeting, and his skills in printing and disseminating written material meant that he would not be released for a very long time.

"I have grown old in here," he told us. "I expect to die in here, now."

The other prison I visited, was in an even more guarded compound in another part of the city. There, a radical and active priest in the reform movement, Father Ed de la Torre, had been held in solitary confinement for many months.

He was internationally known for his writing, his activism and charismatic leadership, so visits were even more strictly controlled than in the main jail.

We learned of his situation through his elderly mother, an amazingly powerful and spiritual woman we all knew as Mommy de la Torre. She was little, fierce and extremely life-affirming, and she organised the visit, saying we were "cousins." Ed's conditions of incarceration were marginally better than for the bulk of the prisoners, but not much, and his mother had to visit him weekly with food and clean clothes. On this occasion she took us along with her.

We talked to Father Ed for thirty minutes or so, eyed suspiciously by two young guards who thankfully did not speak English.

"What are his chances of release?" I asked his mother as we were ushered away when they judged time was up.

"Minimal," she replied, "But we understand it is God's will that he remains here for now. He is here to give spiritual comfort and support to those poor young boys."

"What young boys? He is kept in solitary confinement. There are no other prisoners with him."

"I mean the guards of course. He is with them constantly and can be a huge help to them, as they are so compromised working for the government. But they will think they have little choice in the matter. They are as trapped as he is."

Mommy de la Torre kept pigs on some land she owned. She had a number of breeding sows, all kept in beautiful concrete sheds. We visited, and someone commented that the pigs had better housing than the people.

"True!" she said, "but they need to be sheltered from the sun and rain more than we do."

Her project to support the families of political prisoners centred round a piggy bank idea with a difference. After the sows gave birth, Mommy de la Torre would give a healthy, weaned piglet to a needy family, often where the breadwinner was in jail. The family would take the piglet home, and raise it for six months or so, on household scraps and foraged fruit and grass. Then they could sell it to the butcher, and return to see Mommy de la Torre. They paid about 10% of their selling price back to her, to be given another piglet to raise for meat, and could start again. The piglet money went into the central fund to keep the project afloat.

"Each pig sold will be enough to pay a child's school fees for the year. Many families rely on the pigs just to cover school fees."

Several years later, Mommy travelled to the UK to speak about human rights concerns in the Philippines and she stayed with our family for a few days. She shared an avid interest in poultry keeping with my husband, and said on the final day of her visit, "I see, David, you are a landless peasant. I will pray that God grants you a field before you die."

Now we look out over our acre or two, in our North Yorkshire smallholding, where David keeps his thirteen hen huts, and see that her prayer was answered for us! She was an inspirational figure to all who met her.

Many other Christians in the Philippines seemed like messengers of a truer, more genuine understanding of what the faith is supposed to be about. They shone out from the huge smoky mountain rubbish dump, where we visited a little church built on and from the rubbish, for example, and also in the slums which edged cheek by jowl with the extremely wealthy areas. Many of these people were fearless, feisty nuns, who had been emboldened by the reforms of the Second Vatican Council, to live out the gospel in the heart of the people's own poor communities.

One such nun took us on a little tour round some of the worst housing in Asia, where we had to continually jump over open sewers, but where people had hung up sparkling clean white shirts to dry in the sun. Generally, the people achieved marvellous results from laundry done in cold water with home-made soap, and created food cooked on paint-tins filled with sawdust, the only fuel they could afford.

We visited such a group of washerwomen, who collected piles of dirty laundry from rich people. They washed, dried and somehow managed to iron them all, and carried them back for a dollar a load. Afterwards, the sister said, "Right, now let's see the other side of Manila!"

She took us to one of the huge Western hotels catering for international business, and top-end tourists. The carpark was packed with Mercedes saloons, and when we went inside, we entered an elevator bigger than many of the family homes we had stayed in.

On the floor of the lift was a thick multi-coloured piled carpet. It bore the words. "Hello, this is Monday. Have a nice day." I realised that they changed the carpet each morning to reassure their inebriated guests what day of the week it was.

We then walked round the swimming pool area and the nun told us how the piped music system accompanying us with pop songs also was directed under water. If you dived in, you could still hear your music.

Yet, all round the perimeter wall of this famous hotel, people had made use of this one solid structure to construct their own shelters. These were flimsy little plastic, bamboo and occasionally corrugated tin structures, maybe six by six feet, where they lived, slept, raised their children and in some cases earned their living by tiny shops and businesses.

I understood then, the causes for so much civil unhappiness, and the rise of the People's Party, which in those days, the mid-1980s, was hoping to transform the way things worked or didn't work in the Philippines.

One of the most heart-breaking breakfasts I have ever attended was in Manila, during those hot steamy days in October 1985. A woman called Nellie, articulate, immaculate and well organised in the Filipina manner, showed me over the scheme run by her Methodist Church foundation to help prostitutes by training them for other jobs.

They sat, a few bored girls, either at typewriters or in the "beauty salon" where they were learning to cut hair or apply nail varnish. One sensed the work could only be one rain drop in a desert of misery. Nellie, whose husband was a senior Bishop and general secretary of the Philippine Council of Churches, said fiercely, "The gentle and devoutly religious girls of the Philippines, how are they being made to work now? How are they being marketed abroad by this government? Why, as expendable sexual toys or as domestic slaves. We are becoming known simply as a nation of whores and housemaids!"

Sophie, an English volunteer who worked with her in the scheme, filled in some details.

"In Subic alone, the port where the American nuclear submarines are based, we know there are over twenty-five thousand prostitutes. I did research into where they came from, and I found that over two thirds were from the poorest, most easterly islands where the annual family income is rarely more than US$100 a year.

"When I started the research two years ago, the average age of the girls was fifteen years. Now we are finding, as we are going round the night clubs of Manila that it is rapidly dropping to eleven or twelve years of age. The owners recruit them from the villages, use them for a maximum of six months and then fling them out. On several occasions, the children were simply killed and their bodies thrown in the river."

"Why?" I asked, rather vacuously.

"Because after six months they may catch AIDS and the other diseases the men bring with them. The tourists come to the Philippines for virgins and they certainly like the girls the younger the better. They are all afraid of AIDS now."

My blood ran cold, as the old phrase went, and I ached even more when we welcomed in three of the very children she was describing, two young girls of maybe twelve or thirteen and a small boy of nine. They had all been rescued that very weekend from a bar in the city centre and were like frightened deer. They nibbled at the pastries, and we all tried to reassure them.

"Will they be able to be reunited with their families? Can they find their way home?" I asked, but the staff at the centre were pessimistic.

"It tends to be a one-way street. There is not often a way back. We will look for foster parents, and build them a new life, once they are healed and we have removed the risk of disease, but they may already be HIV positive."

This was in 1985. Thirty-five years later I can tell you the same story, in different countries, with different generations of children, but it is the very same story. Small children prop up the economy of bars all over Asia, Africa, and the Americas, as well as Europe.

Marcos, with his vicious but logical priorities spent 60% of the Philippine entire health budget for one year, building the most prestigious heart hospital in Asia. But nobody apart from the over-fed billionaires needed it. Outside in the streets, the typhoid, dysentery and tuberculosis steadily grew worse, as, of course, did the sufferings of his little prostitutes, 'daintily' advertised on the government tourist brochures.

When I came home from the Philippines, I was sufficiently nauseated by what I had seen of child sex trafficking that fighting it has remained a priority campaign for me ever since. There is nothing as beautiful as the sound of children laughing and chatting together, and there is nothing so painful to hear as the sobbing noise of a child whose innocence has been raped.

One final thought, of course, is that this is a global issue, and very much one for us here in the UK. I knew of a thirteen-year-old girl who had been so excited when she was pursued and entrapped into a relationship by a nineteen-year-old. He used her as a sex toy for months, repeatedly abusing her day after day, until he got bored, and casually dropped her like a brick, roaring off on his motorbike after someone who was fresher meat. She told her best friend at school, but was too scared to tell her parents. I don't think the emotional and physical abuse she suffered was so very different from that endured by the girls I met in Manila.

CHAPTER

8

Fragrant Harbour
1984 Hong Kong

After my weeks in the Philippines, I was asked to take a side trip to Hong Kong, to visit the detention camps of the Vietnamese "boat people." This was some nine years after the main exodus when the war ended in 1975, but Hong Kong was still processing its aftermath. Compared to the sauna-like humidity of Manila, stepping off the plane in Hong Kong was like receiving an intake of cool, pure oxygen. Of course, many of the locals didn't share my view.

Two million people fled Vietnam between the end of the war in 1975 and almost 800,000 had left by sea, most heading for Hong Kong, Malaysia or Indonesia. Many died as their boats sank at sea or were attacked by pirates from Thailand. But sizeable numbers did survive, picked up by cargo boats, often just before they capsized in the South China seas.

While the majority were eventually taken in by the US, Australia and Canada, a few settled in the UK, where a small but vibrant community developed. Margaret Thatcher had been vehemently opposed to receiving refugees, which meant that those who wished to emigrate found the doors into the UK increasingly difficult to open.

Working through the Hong Kong Red Cross and the local Council of Churches, our charity provided case workers, English language teaching, and help for the many very small children struggling to live in the great barracks which formed a refugee detention centre on a smaller island. I was very cordially received by a senior official and escorted across the bay in his power launch.

"It is a very slow and tedious business for most of the prisoners, sorry, detainees, as they seek to gain refugee status and visas to emigrate. Hong Kong has been very conscientious about doing our duty and processing them, but as the years go on, other countries are more resistant to helping. The flow of boats has lessened though in the last year or so."

"So, the boat people are confined within the camp?"

"Yes, we cannot risk them escaping into the city."

So, he was right, his slip of the tongue revealed the reality, that all the boat people in Vietnam were in fact prisoners, serving an indeterminate sentence, and not permitted to leave the compound or seek work in the city.

My guide had been a senior official in the prison service. He was very tall for a Chinese person, and obviously carried a large amount of authority. While we crossed the bay, he told me interesting things about the different ethnicities within China, north and south, east and west. He had also worked in immigration control between Hong Kong and Mainland China.

"We were constantly finding people trying to immigrate into Hong Kong. One couple walked across the border from China into Kowloon wearing full evening dress. The man had on a dinner jacket and his wife had a long gown, fur stole with high heels. They told us they had been told everyone wore clothes like this in Hong Kong so they had expected to blend in un-noticed."

I was given a tour of the camp and allowed to talk freely to the Vietnamese, who clustered round me. The camp was clean but very crowded, with bunkbeds tiered up to four in a tower. People had turned them into mini capsule homes. The general atmosphere was very depressing. Years of confinement had aged many of the younger people into a desperate acquiescence, and I could see hope was dying in their eyes that they would ever get out.

Since then, I have visited several refugee camps in various countries, and also talked to many asylum seekers in the UK, and the over-riding sense one has is the pointless waste of talent, energy and ability pinned down by systems which prevent people working, rebuilding their lives productively and flourishing in a way which would have helped their host countries.

Of course, the bulk of refugees live in Africa, where neighbouring countries to conflict zones have received, even welcomed, migrants fleeing war or starvation. I have talked to young people who have moved south on foot from Sudan and Somalia into northern Kenya and Uganda, and have been well received, educated and supported to carve out new productive futures. But for others, escaping the terror in their own country was to be only the start of their miseries.

Years later, revisiting California to write a book on justice and peace groups there, I stayed in the Vietnamese heartland of a section of Orange County which became known as Little Saigon. The strip malls of medical clinics, dentist surgeries, manicure salons, and a host of Asian food shops showed the vibrancy of the culture, now a fusion of Vietnamese and American life, made possible, and certainly enabled by a humane immigration policy of the seventies and eighties.

One of my friends, who was an art teacher, had seventeen different nationalities represented in her classes, which attracted students whose English was still minimal. She had one sixteen-year-old pupil, who learned English rapidly, graduated High School with a 4.0 grade point average, which meant she had top marks in all subjects, and gained a scholarship to study medicine. She is now a top-flight physician specialising in paediatrics.

It is the stories of people like her which keep one's hopes alive. But how many potential brain surgeons or engineers have died trying to cross the ocean, whether it is the Mediterranean, the Aegean or the China Seas? The complacency with which we have learned to hear the appalling death tolls from drowning in recent years is astounding.

After my daytrip into despair in the boat people's detention camp, my visit to Hong Kong had two other main events. The first was a service at St John's Anglican Cathedral, where afterwards I met with a group of young women from the Philippines, who were all working as maids in Hong Kong. They had been given a room and refreshments on a Sunday afternoon to have a fellowship meeting with each other, if they were allowed the hour or two off and allowed to leave their employer's house and flats, which for many was a forbidden activity.

Their stories echoed the realities I had encountered in Manila and other cities in the Philippines. No-one wanted to be in Hong Kong. No-one wanted to work as a maid for

English or Chinese families, who treated them occasionally well, but mostly as virtual slaves or objects, like a human vacuum cleaner.

They came because this was the only way they could afford to keep their children in school, or a roof over their parents' heads. What I thought was economically crazy, was that many of the women were highly educated and professionally qualified. But they could still earn more as a maid in Hong Kong or Singapore, than as a doctor in Manila.

"I am a qualified dentist," one woman confided in me. "But, of course, I would not dare to confess this to my Madam. She has little education, and would fire me if she knew. So, I pretend I know nothing, to save her face."

These girls were lucky, in at least their employers let them out on a Sunday, to attend Mass and meet up with their friends. Many, including my friend Georgina, were not so fortunate. When she started work in Singapore a few years later, her "Madam" told her, "Oh, no, I do not allow any days off. Maybe, after you have worked a year for me, then you may have a free day."

My final visit in Hong Kong, or "Fragrant Harbour" as the original Chinese meaning is said to be, was to travel up the highest mountain in the territory. This was a beautiful interlude. The track went higher and higher, and the air became clearer and sweeter as we climbed. Hong Kong did have many fragrant corners, and when we reached near the summit, we could look down on all the chaotic and noisy commerce and high-rise buildings below us, but also enjoy the pine trees and smell the flowers.

I had been advised to visit the ashram at the top of the hill, where a very elderly ascetic and, you might say, rather eccentric, English couple lived a life of Christian- Buddhist simplicity, praying for the city below and holding it up to God. They had one or two other people living with them, and we shared a vegetarian meal served in small bamboo bowls.

They had previously been based in India. The wife wore a sari, I remember. I have tried to recall their names, and research the centre, but sadly without success. So, they remain anonymous.

But there definitely was a strongly spiritual sense of engagement up there, close to the clouds. While the noise and bustle of the city seemed far away, my day at the ashram gave me the strength to process all the challenges I had seen below, as well as the dose of human complexity and compassion I had also witnessed in the Philippines. It was a gift, which I received gratefully.

I have never visited mainland China, but one has to feel a humility in the face of such an ancient, recorded civilisation. Two significant women in my life did have closer connections to it though, and the first, surprisingly was my American host mother from the time I had lived with her back in 1970 to 1971.

In later life she began to travel outside the USA, and these trips included visits to China and the Far East. She would tell me about the people she had met, and made me realise how radically her ideas had changed from the times we had argued when I lived under her roof. Her travels certainly softened her previously hard-line views about communism, and East Asians in general. She told me how surprised and even shocked she was by discovering the Chinese trains were divided into first- and second-class carriages, and that the first class were quite luxurious.

She felt guilty being an affluent American tourist in China, when most people had so little and was particularly overwhelmed by the people crushing into Beijing's main bookshop, all desperate for reading matter and educational textbooks. It stood in stark contrast with the pulp newspapers and soft porn and cartoon comic-strip magazines which the American public was given to read, she commented.

She was also amazed to see the bright, beautifully embroidered clothing of so many children, cosseted and spoilt, but more and more frequently growing up without brothers and sisters.

In the seventies and eighties, the Chinese national obsession with birth control was at its height, and she also discovered their droll sense of humour. She was travelling in a remote western province and noticed lots of pomegranate trees. Had these trees been imported originally from the Middle East, along the silk route?

"Yes," replied her guide. "That's right. But for many hundreds of years now they have been a favourite fruit in China. We always serve them at wedding feasts."

"Why is that?"

"Because the pomegranate is a symbol of fertility. Many pips inside, many children to bless the marriage."

"Oh," hesitated my host mother. "But what happens these days? Do you still serve pomegranates at weddings?"

The guide smiled a little sadly. "No, we no longer serve this fruit at weddings, but we have found a good substitute. Now we serve peaches!"

I had another good friend who told me of her experiences teaching English in China just after the Cultural Revolution. She was mainly surprised by how friendly and helpful her students were. They invited her to their rooms for meals and told her she was always to contact them immediately if she had any problems.

"Why are you so kind to me?" she asked them when she knew them better.

They replied, "Because you are alone here and have no family. Everyone knows that in China, family is crucial. You cannot operate unless you have a family network to support you and work the system to get what you need."

She also had some interesting experiences which illustrated the isolation of the country in those days.

Firstly, the apartments shooting up in the cities very rarely had private bathrooms and toilets, so finding accommodation near to a public toilet was almost as important as locating the nearest Tube station or bus stop would be in London. No-one served drinks after 7.00pm either, as they understood the challenge of a full bladder after midnight.

My friend also needed an injection and went to a large health clinic to receive it. There were no private consultation or treatment rooms, so in a corner of a huge hall in the hospital, she was asked to drop her pants and bend over to be injected in the backside.

"An enormous uproar of excitement started," she recalled. "The cry went up, "White lady's bottom. Come and see white lady's bottom!" And there was a mad rush of excited, but quite innocent sightseers crowding round her to catch a glimpse of this exotic thing."

I only glimpsed the enormity of China as a series of shadowy hills across the bay from Hong Kong, but it has remained a mysterious destination I still hope to explore. The head-teacher of my girls' high school, the woman who had started all my global wonderings by kick-starting my application to become an exchange student, was actually born in Western China in the 1930s, when her father was a missionary there. On retirement in the 1980s, she wanted to return as a visitor, despite dreading finding out what had happened to the church he had founded. It must have been destroyed through the subsequent Communist revolution of 1948, and then the Cultural Revolution. Surely no-one could have survived the great purges.

"But when I reached the village where I was born, a ninety-year-old man, who had been my father's assistant came to meet me, saying he remembered the day I was born! And the Church, the actual Church was still going, with an active congregation. I just could not believe it. I asked him how they had survived persecution. 'Oh,' he said, 'Yes there were some troubles for a while. But we made it through. Everything is fine now. No bother. We just carried on'".

In one sense, time had stood still. The human spirit can prove remarkably resilient, and we are adaptable. It is obviously one reason for our species spreading all over the globe. We migrate.

When I arrived back home in England, my little family had put up a welcome banner saying "Welcome Home!" There had been a typhoon in the Philippines it seemed, which I had not even noticed, but which had been widely reported by the BBC, so they had been extremely worried for me. My younger son who was only five, had also claimed to his father he wasn't sure he could remember my face.

"There is a photo of Mummy in the upstairs bedroom. Go and take a look," my husband had said. So, my son ran up the stairs and then came down again, beaming. He remembered me after all.

CHAPTER
9

In the Shadow of Pinochet
1987 Chile

It was to be another three years before I travelled again for work, this time to a very different part of the world, Chile and then Bolivia. I seemed to have an unfortunate habit of chasing dictatorships, so this time it was to the Chile of General Pinochet, pal of Mrs Thatcher, and scourge of all those struggling for social reform and relief from poverty.

When we visited, in 1987, far too many of his citizens were incarcerated in prison, sent into internal exile, or simply disposed of, never to be seen again. Priests, poets, nuns, especially young people – no-one was secure. It was the nearest thing to a fascist state that I have ever experienced, where violence ruled, and the people who lived in the poor favelas, or informal conurbations round the outskirts of the cities, lived in constant fear of night-time shoot-outs and brutal repression.

An example of this was what happened in the informal community of La Victoria, on the outskirts of Santiago. It was a very poor area, where the houses were mostly made of wood, with rickety doors and windows, and people's incomes were as insecure as their housing.

Men would carry their toolboxes with their trade painted on the outside, "Carpenter," "Mason," "Roofer," for example. They would then gather at dawn in the marketplace, for contractors to come by and hire them by the day, as and where they might be needed. Wages were minimal, and the weaker looking, or heaven forbid, those who arrived late, generally went without work and their families stayed hungry.

I saw this system in action, and it reminded me forcibly of the Bible story Jesus told about the labourers waiting for work. All needed the same minimal wage, some had work for the whole day, but some were only hired for one or two hours, and some missed out altogether. It was essentially the same power dynamic as today's zero hours' contracts.

The women in La Victoria, as in some other places, supplemented their husband's meagre wages by having cooking clubs called "Ollas Communes." Maybe a dozen or so mothers would bring whatever they had to add to the pot, some chicken wings perhaps, potatoes, vegetables of any sorts, anything they could offer, and it was all turned into a large soupy stew, boiled up and then divided out into the vessels brought from home. This meal would be the family dinner. It saved on fuel, and seriously improved the nutrition for each set of hungry children, otherwise faced with some noodles and maybe half an onion.

The women told me of a recent police raid on one such gathering, as group meetings were forbidden under the police state. "The police stole our large pot of food, and confiscated it. They also took away the large spoon we used to stir the soup. We followed them to the police station, demanding our pot back, which they eventually did, but they had eaten all our stew! They also kept our spoon, saying it was used too much for agitation!"

This was very oppressive policing, but it had its humorous side. Much less humorous was the evidence everywhere of the brutality these people endured. Their houses, the community centre and even the church buildings were pock-marked with bullet holes. When the armed militias working for the government came round at night, they would often fire indiscriminately at the houses, strafing the streets with machine gun fire or high velocity bullets.

One such bullet had killed the local priest, a missionary from Belgium, as he sat at his desk reading from the psalms. His house, as poor as others in the street had been turned into a shrine, and we visited, seeing his blood still spilled over the psalm he had been reading. A bitter follow-up to this story had just occurred.

We were shown sacks of dried milk donated by his supporting churches back in Belgium. Before they could be distributed to feed under-nourished children, the military police had returned again, ripped them open and tried to contaminate them as much as possible. Such hatred for the poor in one's own country and for those supporting them was a hallmark of the Pinochet regime.

The women's groups told their stories, rather like those who created the Bayeux tapestry, through the most exquisite little cloth pictures, called 'arpilleras'. These are well known across South American as a folk art-form which tourists like to buy. The only difference in Chile was that the stories portrayed were of death, torture, resilience and defiance against the government. They were strangely powerful, a gentle art-form, using scraps of cloth and embroidery turned into a first-hand testimony of lost children, dead husbands, tortured mothers.

I can bear witness to the torture inflicted on women. I went to a centre, in a Methodist church schoolroom, where survivors of prison torture met weekly to try to deal with their ordeals and the memories they could not erase. About twenty women, young and old were gathered together. A young man, a member of the national Ballet company, was with them, giving them coaching in physical confidence. It was an amazing sight.

He was teaching them to stand, not cower. In prison, if you raised your eyes you could very easily get your teeth kicked in, and as a result many of the women present could no longer maintain eye contact with strangers or anyone in authority.

He showed them how to stand and walk around the room freely, greeting each other with confidence. Some found this very difficult. He then demonstrated that a policeman standing back on his heels with his arms folded in front of him, as so many did, would actually be physically quite unstable, and a light push from in front could knock him over. I remember how some of the women found this very entertaining, not that they were likely to try it anytime soon.

We stayed on for the next session, an art class, and I was very touched by how many of the women painted small houses, with flowers in front, symbols of home and happiness. The ones who spoke up told us in Spanish, that one or two of the class remained completely silent about their prison experiences, finding it too traumatic to even speak of the rapes, the sexual violence using electric cattle prods, and worse.

The leader of the group said, "We tell them that we all

know how it was, that everything they have suffered, we have experienced too, so they should not be afraid or shamed. We know that if they keep coming here, one day they will be able to speak about what happened to them, and then they will start to heal."

These women, many of whom had been widowed by the regime or lost their sons and daughters in the terrible purges and shootings were some of the bravest people I have ever met.

Santiago was, in many ways, a beautiful city, European and cosmopolitan in its feel, and for the middle and upper classes and those who refused to take any part in the movement against the Pinochet regime, I am sure it was a pleasant place to live. I remember the classical music they played in the metro stations, and the cheerful laughter in the boulevard restaurants, but there was always a dark side, a terror lurking below the surface.

From Santiago we went to the hillside communities round the port of Valparaiso, and here again were privileged to see the contrast between the lives of the rich and the poor, the five percent and the ninety-five percent. Here again were the poor wooden houses without proper sanitation, the unmade roads twisting up the hillsides, and the queues of skilled craftsmen begging for work.

In one such community, I visited a "Rainy Day Club" which intrigued me. The leader explained. "Any day it rains, not too often in these parts, but maybe three or four times a month, we stop doing what we normally do, and bake bread and cakes. These we sell in the market, and all the money we make we club together into a fund. Then, if we have a husband who falls sick and who cannot work, we have enough in the kitty to support his family for a few days."

"How is it going?" I asked. "Have you managed to cover your group's needs?"

"Yes," the leader said, "We had a little surplus by the end of the year, and the weather was so nice we decided to hire a mini-bus and take our children to the beach. There is a famous resort near here on the coast we would like to go to. We arrived at the beach but the security guards told us we weren't permitted on the beach, that it was reserved for rich people, and Argentinian people who come across from the East. It was in fact a public beach, but they would not allow us on as we all looked shabby."

"So what did you do?"

"We gave up the argument and took our kids further down the shoreline. The sands weren't as good, but we had a picnic on the seaside, and enjoyed ourselves. It was like a real day's holiday!"

They had real spirit, those ladies of the Rainy-Day Club.

While on the coast we also visited a renowned priest, Father Alfredo, a locally famous leader in the Resistance movement, who had been exiled for seven years down to the southernmost tip of Chile, a barren, very cold corner of this amazingly long and thin country.

Against all the odds he had battled with the government, and their allies, the conservative Church authorities to return to his original parish. He was eventually allowed back but forbidden from preaching, so he had opened a centre to teach people how to garden better and grow more food, and I remember the vitality and ingenuity of many of his schemes to improve the health of the sandy soil and grow more crops.

The rubber tyre gardens, the hanging baskets made from old cans, all these reminded me of the Philippines. In fact, many of the gardens I have seen round the world, community efforts springing up in most unpromising locations, have shown the same irrepressible energy and hope. Father Alfredo's garden was a real embodiment of Christianity as I understand it, and it lifted my depression after visiting and being with so many folks who had suffered much at the hands of truly unpleasant officials and people who had taken power illegally.

The sad thing is, repression and the violent suppression of basic human rights, ultimately can crush the spirit of a whole nation. But the good thing is, the human spirit of cooperation, unselfish communitarianism and the hope that something better is always just round the corner can keep things alive when the ground seems stony and unproductive.

One person I met, years later, reaffirmed that for me. Let's call her Sister Isabel. A British Roman Catholic nun, she had worked in Chile for many years, and, in the dark days of the Pinochet regime, had done much to smuggle innocent people away from the military police who came searching for them.

She would help them hide in her convent, slip them away from the city, and give them funds in order to leave the country. She saved many people, men and women, young people and students from the torture chambers of the regime over the years.

But one day, the police came for her. The head of her religious order was given a tip-off that her arrest was imminent, and she instructed Sister Isabel to leave on a flight back to England, immediately, no arguing.

"If you don't go now, they will catch you and torture you. You know too many names, have helped too many people. You will probably break down eventually and put other people's lives in jeopardy. So you must go."

Sister Isabel had worked in Chile for many years, and all those she loved were there, and still in great danger. She told me it literally broke her heart to fly away, back to England and to safety. Because she was so traumatised, it was many years before she could even speak a word of her experiences in Santiago.

I met her when we were both guest speakers at a Justice and Peace conference years later, by which time, she could talk about her years in South America and bear truthful witness to the torture and killings she had seen first-hand.

She was delighted to discover I had visited Chile the same time as she had worked there. She had a wicked sense of humour, and a kind of "devil may care" attitude which I liked very much.

We had a free afternoon during the conference, and she asked me if I'd like to go with her into the nearest town and buy Christmas presents for all the elderly sisters in her Convent or mother house. I agreed, as it seemed a fun project, and we took my car.

When I looked for a parking place, Sister Isabel poured scorn on my obedience to officialdom. "I never bother about double yellow lines anymore," she proclaimed. "When you've had to run for your life from military death squads, parking tickets aren't worth bothering about."

But I parked legally somewhere and we went through the market town looking for presents.

"How much money do you have to spend?" I asked.

"Five Pounds."

"Oh, and how many sisters do you want to buy presents for?"

"Ten."

This seemed an impossible target. But Sister Isabel taught me a thing or two about shopping that afternoon. We stuck to charity shops of course, and emerged from the last one, with presents for each of the nuns. Bath cubes, a hot water bottle cover, cosy mittens, bars of soap, a little china saucer, things like this which each cost no more than 50 pence, along with some wrapping paper and little tags, came within her budget. Each sister would get her own gift on Christmas morning, and Isabel was content.

We returned to the conference where tea and fruitcake was being served, very happy shoppers. I think that was the sweetest Christmas shopping expedition I have ever made. I just hoped someone in her Order had bought her a present, too.

CHAPTER
10

A Bread Bin for a Baby
1987 Bolivia

La Paz in Bolivia is one of the very highest cities in the world, located around 12000 feet above sea level, and the lack of oxygen is noticeable as soon as one lands in the airport. The locals swear by coca tea, and will brew it for you as soon as you book into a hotel. This green leaf, from which cocaine can be refined and produced, helps your heart and lungs make better use of what little air there is. It is nature's medicine, they say, and everywhere you go, people are chewing the leaves of the coca tree in the corner of their mouths.

La Paz is also very cold, even in summer at night, and the local Quechua and Aymara women are by no means as plump as they appear, because they dress in umpteen flannel petticoats to keep themselves warm as they stand on the pavements, selling whatever they can, including dried dead animals used in rituals and worship of the earth mother goddess. The ubiquitous bowler hats so many women also wear came, so the story goes, out of an original shipment from a ship which ran aground in the late nineteenth century on its way north to San Francisco, bearing thousands of hats which washed ashore.

The local Bolivian and Peruvian men weren't so impressed, but their women folk loved them, and they all started wearing them. When the original consignment was used up, then the country directly imported more hats from Europe which were landed in a more organised manner than simply washed ashore (I'm not sure if this is totally true, but it's a good story).

After Chile, the political atmosphere in Bolivia was noticeably less chilly than the weather. Outside our hotel window, I saw a female doughnut seller on the street corner vociferously arguing with a policeman who wanted her to clear the pavement. Never would she have dared to do such a thing in Chile, but finally, in exasperation, she picked up one of her doughnuts and threw it at his head. It him squarely on the nose, and with that onslaught, he retreated from the battle and left her to her pitch.

La Paz was nothing if not lively. A demonstration and a march from one of the miners' unions was disrupting traffic near the town hall. The men from the silver and tin mines were striking for a living wage and more safety equipment and they were desperate. Their banners were lively, but their faces looked pinched and poor.

Street traders were everywhere. From morning to night, the streets were full of stalls and pitches, often with people selling tiny objects, impossible to sell for any profit. At ten o'clock at night I saw a small girl of maybe eleven years old, shivering outside a cinema in front of a small collection of the hair decorations we used to call bobby dazzlers, silver stars on springs. I could not imagine anyone emerging from the late film wanting to buy one, but she sat there, in her navy school uniform, hour after hour, an exercise book, open on the rug beside her. She was obviously trying to complete her homework while she was on duty.

One little tradesman I will never forget was a small boy of about eight years old, who had a shoe-shine business. A wooden box with his brushes and a tiny tin of polish, hung from his shoulder, and he had an apprentice with him, his little brother who could only have been about five. Both children were ragged, and their faces were burnt with frost bite.

I was wearing stout leather boots and they followed me up and down the street asking if they could clean them for me. Many of the tourists had abandoned leather shoes for canvas trainers, so it was a buyer's market for shoe-shining. I finally agreed and put my foot up on the little ramp created from the upside-down brush box.

The child cleaned and polished away with vigour and made a very good job, while his little brother held the brushes. I then paid him the local equivalent of about twenty-five pence, and was surprised when he said, "Sorry, I have no change." My translator told me his words and explained, "You have given him fifty times the normal rate for the job. They normally get less than a cent."

I was so shocked and shook my head at the boy's offer of change, saying, "Go on, take it, it's yours!" The look on both the children's faces was as though I had given them a wonderful present, and they ran off up the hill together. I later saw them at one of the stalls which were selling meat empanadas, so their takings obviously went straight into their tummies. I was glad for that, at least.

La Paz had many a similar educational experience for us, but our most touching encounter was at an independent orphanage, supported by some of the wealthier ladies in the city. I had seen a film about this place on the flight coming up from Chile and wanted to see it for myself. So, we asked our Council of Churches host about it.

"Is it true that there is an orphanage here with a hole in the wall like a bank night-safe, where people leave unwanted babies?"

"Yes, surely. In fact, we passed it last night as we walked home down the street outside the cinema. If you would like to go, then I can call and make a request."

So, the following day, we visited the orphanage, run by its Director, a very resilient Catholic sister, with the help mainly of a group of teenage girls, who had been at the orphanage since they were children. Between them they ran a commercial bakery, rising at 4 am to make bread and sell it to the shops and traders. In this way the care needed for the abandoned younger children was paid for.

The sister was very friendly, and gave us a demonstration of how the baby receiver worked. It was just like a bread-bin, the sort with a swing lid. There was room inside for a baby if you opened the metal lid, and when a child was placed inside, then you could ring the bell and run away without being detected. One of the older girls' duties was to sleep on a cot in the room behind the "baby safe" and retrieve the child if the bell rang.

"Is it ever used these days?" I asked, for it seemed a relic from a by-gone era.

We were told babies were originally just left on the orphanage steps, where, if they were not found before morning, they had usually perished from the cold. Hence the baby safe had been installed decades before.

"Oh yes," exclaimed the Sister Director. "Two nights ago, at 10.15 pm, a very poorly baby girl was left in it. In fact, this has caused a small financial crisis. There will be no dessert for any of the children for the rest of the month, as the new child had to be rushed to hospital for immediate emergency care, and we have to pay a large bill. This is surely the reason she was handed to us, to save her life, for her parents obviously could not afford the money to take her to hospital."

My heart gave a shudder, for we had walked down that street at just that time. While we were strolling along, someone in the shadows had been going through the agony of relinquishing their child.

"Will she survive?"

"Yes, she will survive, and if the parents do not come back for her, then we will put her up for adoption. We do arrange international adoptions here. We are licensed by the government, as there are so many orphaned or abandoned babies, especially girls; our country doesn't seem able to care for them here. Come with me, and I will show you how it works."

We entered a bright nursery, with maybe twenty bouncing baby chairs on the floor, each chair having a little girl, under twelve months, wearing snug 'baby-gro' sleep suits, and being cared for by the nursery nurses. Coming out of a side room, clutching some papers came a very well-dressed Italian couple.

The woman's eyes were full of tears, and we watched as they were directed to one of the little bouncing chairs, and given a smiling baby with the characteristic sticking up hair of the native Bolivian children. As they took the child in their arms, you could see the intense emotion going through their minds. It was almost enough to make us cry.

The Director was anxious we didn't get the idea she was selling babies. "Each couple has to undergo rigorous checks. They have to be good Catholics, and they cannot have any children already of their own. They must both stay in Bolivia for three months before adopting, so they learn all about the culture of the child, and prove how committed they are."

"Do they get to choose their child?"

"No, we simply give them the child who has been given a clean bill of health, is now very healthy and vaccinated, and ready to leave. No parents object to this, as they all see it as a gift from God."

I had many more questions, and not a few doubts about this system. But the room was full of the sweetest children, for whom this might be their only chance of life outside an institution. I did like the Director, who seemed to have her head screwed on, and coped with enormous stress of feeding fifty children every day. She really was like the old woman who lived in a shoe.

I had brought to South America with me a package of linen tea towels from the Cheshire Diocese Mothers' Union, which I had been giving out as small souvenir thank you gifts, and I considered her a worthy recipient.

She asked what the writing said, and I told her it was "Mothers' Union", which my host translated into Spanish for her.

"What a wonderful idea! I wish we had a Mothers' Union in our country. It's just what we need here too. If mothers had power, then we could change the world!"

But she obviously dreamed of a much more vociferous and radical idea of a union than the gentle lobbying and local fellowship groups of the UK Mothers' Union.

I have often thought of that little baby about to be taken off to Italy, and prayed that her life would fulfil that early promise of love and care. If she is alive today, she must be thirty –two, perhaps with a family of her own.

From La Paz, we were taken by one of the ubiquitous Toyota land-cruisers through lands even higher in altitude, to breathlessly meet with the people struggling to make a living on some of the highest ground on the planet, up on the windy slopes of the Alto Plano. Christian Aid had funded a seemingly impossible project there to import British dairy cattle, black and white cows of the sort more at home in Cheshire than out in Bolivia, to provide a core herd of heavy milk producers. We were off to visit it.

The local project manager was a veterinarian, a charming man with a deeply alarming hobby of taxidermy. He told us proudly he had stuffed and mounted an example of virtually every mammal, bird, insect and reptile found in Bolivia.

Unfortunately, what might have formed a national collection in a wealthier country had not been adopted by any museum and given a home, so they were all installed in his own, modest apartment. Finally losing patience, his wife had left him, taking the children with her, and his only living companion was his dog, who definitely looked very scared.

His living quarters were absolutely packed to the ceiling with dead, stuffed animals and birds, including a great Andean condor, and we all jumped in alarm when the dog walked in. Everywhere smelt strongly of formaldehyde. Our host opened cabinet after cabinet to show us even more specimens, impaled butterflies, moths and even spiders.

Outside this home of horrors, he was a very polite and pleasant man, and he drove us up the mountains in his jeep to visit the Quechua subsistence farmers, a few thousand metres even higher. The air was as thin as tissue paper, and the sky was a deep, frozen blue.

We politely inspected the dairy unit, with its well-housed and sheltered but rather bewildered herd of Friesian cows, and then drove on, up to the village to meet some of the farmers involved. Llamas and alpacas browsed the sparse vegetation. It is interesting that now these have been imported and bred in large numbers in the far lusher pastures of the UK, so maybe animal colonialism has developed in both directions.

One leading farmer was very friendly, his wife equally so, but their first, quite fierce question to us, via the interpreter, surprised us, being, "What denomination are you?"

This was unexpected, but they explained that they were very keen Seventh Day Adventists, converted by an American missionary called Sandra. The woman's adorable baby, slung round her shoulders in a multi-coloured blanket, had been named after this visitor. Their new faith obviously meant a lot to them, but I was very sad to see how denominational differences and disputes in countries so far from Bolivia, and really so irrelevant to their own cultural heritage had been allowed to gain importance to them.

Baby Sandra and I took to each other immediately. Her mother wore a small brown bowler hat precariously balanced over her long-braided hair, and Sandra had a floppy cotton sunhat to protect her little round face from frostbite and sunburn, which affected most local children simultaneously.

Our visit obviously attracted a lot of local attention and very soon a group of men gathered to meet and greet, while Sandra's mother disappeared into the two-room house to prepare food for us all. I followed her inside, as I was far more interested in her domestic realities than talking with the men about the potential of milk production. By the use of sign language and my very poor Spanish we had a chat about the menu for lunch.

Essentially it was potatoes, ten years old, dug out of a clamp. They looked unlike any potatoes I had ever seen. How would she cook them?

"Oh, twenty minutes in boiling salted water."

"So, just like potatoes at home then?"

"Yes."

The soil was so thin on the patch outside I wondered how she managed to grow anything, let alone potatoes, but these were obviously tough little tubers who grew in even the most inhospitable country. Bolivia was their native land after all.

Ten-year-old potatoes were meant to be a local delicacy, but were definitely an acquired taste. I had offered to hold Sandra, and kept her close throughout the meal. This was definitely to my advantage. My colleagues and I were each handed enamel dishes piled with rotting, black, ten-year-old potatoes, all nicely boiled, but not exactly transformed by the process.

I tried to bite into one, but immediately wanted to gag. Sandra looked at me with her enormous one-year-old eyes, and indicated she would rather like some too. So, while we chatted with her charming and vivacious mother I secretly passed the potatoes pieces one by one to the baby girl, who munched on them enthusiastically. Cultural diversity at its finest. My male colleagues had no such let-out, and I watched them suffer as they tried to be polite guests and finish their lunch.

As the token woman in the party, I felt I should ask about the role of females in this notoriously macho society. As we met with the village elders, and the project managers I asked a typical 1980s' question.

"How do you involve women in the decision making of your project?"

This was translated into Quechua, and the men were initially very puzzled by it, but then the leading man answered, "Oh yes, our women, they are very important. This one especially!"

He pointed to a little lady, totally swathed in petticoats and wearing several shawls and bowler hat. She was one of the oldest and shortest in the group, certainly well under five-foot-high, and her many shawls and skirts made her look completely spherical. She gave a shy curtsey and put her hand over her mouth in the universal sign for embarrassment at being singled out.

"This one," he continued, "she is our champion footballer!"

"Que?" Surely, we had misheard!

He explained.

"No, here we have a local form of football, which goes from village to village. The first village has a team who kick the ball across the hills to the next village, maybe five or six kilometres.

"When they get there, the receiving team challenges them for the ball, and chases them back to the original village. Whoever has the ball in its possession at the end is the winner. This lady, she is our fastest runner and our best kicker. She is very important to our project!"

All of this in air as thin as that at Everest base camp! I was in total awe, and decided to ask no more questions about feminine empowerment.

One of the biggest barriers to women's empowerment

in Bolivia was the very high rate of illiteracy among the poor communities, which impacted women and girls even more than boys. The final day in the La Paz area was spent visiting an inspirational project up near the airport, where Paulo Freire's teachings about bringing about change through literacy in one's mother tongue had borne great fruit.

A women's group had started a scheme to give its members power through understanding the use of words. They started with the simplest words which had most meaning in their lives. I saw the teaching materials, thin, floppy, hand-printed books, and watched a lesson. The first word taught was "Wawa." What did it mean? Well guess! Say it out loud and you will see.

Ah, it is the local word for baby, the closest thing to each woman in the room, literally, as most had babies nestled against their breasts. The baby makes the crying sound, "wa-wa," and that is what they are called.

The next page had a picture of a llama, another word which everyone knew, and so their vocabulary and ability to read gradually built up.

The teacher was an inspirational woman who told me, "In six months we can get the brightest and most committed young women from total illiteracy up to the level where they are writing a letter of complaint to the local mayor's office about the lack of piped water into our community."

This was inspiring, and, fifteen years later, when I was working in Africa, I was part of a literacy movement called REFLECT, which used almost the same methods (a story told later in this book). The poor communities in Bolivia had even fewer resources than those in Chile, no piped water or electricity, while the great hydro-electric power stations overshadowed their favelas, and the rich had satellite dishes and electric fridges to keep their drinks cool.

No state pension or national insurance against disaster meant that the poor were cruelly exposed to any natural disaster or personal illness. Children were put to work as soon as they could carry a hod of bricks, and babies had to be given up for adoption if they fell ill.

But despite this, the people of the Andes had a huge dignity and stoicism in the face of deprivation. Children seemed to cry very rarely, swaddled like papooses and lying on the ground next to their mothers who tried to sell small items or home-grown vegetables in the market.

Where I saw real misery, and a stripping away of all human dignity, was on my next port of call, down the mountains into the tropical, steamy part of Bolivia, where the great sugar plantations ran as far as the Amazon catchment area, centred on the city of Santa Cruz.

Bolivia is a large country, divided into two very separate geographical regions, the high Andes Mountains to the west, and the low, tropical flat lands to the east. The people are different, as are the languages spoken, and they could be two separate nations. In some ways, only the poverty of the poorest of the poor unites them.

Santa Cruz, our next destination, is a sugar town, the centre of a prosperous region for those who have sugar-cane plantations and the money to farm them or keep cattle. It is a pleasing city, warm and sunny, with open air restaurants and pleasant boulevards reaching out from the central square. We spent a week or so in its environs, enjoying the warmth after the freezing altitude of the mountains, but the poverty I saw there matched anything I have seen in the world.

Our first location was the migrant camps for Quechua and Aymara people who had come from the mountains to cut cane. They were completely wretched, with no facilities apart from wooden shacks where men and women were crammed in, lying on bare trestle benches and not even sheltered from the regular torrential rain which poured through flimsy leaking roofs.

The bosses and owners of the plantations openly despised the mountain people, and made little effort to treat them as fellow citizens. Down in the east area, most people spoke Spanish, and far more than in La Paz were of European descent.

The work was back-breaking, especially for the short and stouter mountain folk, and the pay appalling for long days. As the camps were usually miles from the nearest village, communication with folks back up in the Alto Plano and the chance to educate their children was almost impossible.

Occasionally teachers were allocated to the camps area, but they rarely stayed long, as it was impossible for them to collect their wages through a post-office, which might be twenty miles away, without any public transport to reach it.

We sat with the workers on a Sunday afternoon and listened to their tales of woe. When they had been recruited by the gang-masters, they'd been promised good wages, decent accommodation and medical and educational facilities for their families.

So many had come with their entire family, only to encounter conditions no better than slavery, and were caught in a trap. They had borrowed money to make the six-hundred-mile journey, and could not leave without paying it all back. Everyone we spoke to said they were acutely homesick for their homes up in the high mountains, poor as the conditions were back there, and wished they could return.

But they were paid three months or more in arrears, and often in tokens to spend only in the sugar company store. The mission staff who were fighting for the workers' rights were continually obstructed and harangued by the bosses. This is how it was in the late 1980s. I only hope life is transformed for such workers now, but I wouldn't bet much money on that.

In that area, though, we met some amazing people. The first were connected to a children's farm on the outskirts of Santa Cruz, established twenty years or more before by a religious order to rescue street boys and give them a home and something productive to work for.

When we visited, this farm was a veritable hive of activity, with a pig unit, hundreds of chickens, raised both for eggs and meat, and a large orchard and market garden. Boys, and more recently girls, had been rescued and given a home there on the farm, which also ran its own schools.

We visited on a Saturday, and met an attorney, a young man of maybe twenty-eight or thirty, who practised law in Santa Cruz. He was organising the boys into a football match, and said he came back most weekends to play with them and mentor the older students through their schoolwork.

I asked why he did this, and he replied, "Because I was one of them not so long ago. I was one of the first boys whom Father Juan rescued from the streets, and I will always be grateful to him and the others who gave me a home, a life and a future."

We walked round the whole farm and inspected the facilities, which were excellent. One of the secular managers of the farm told us more about how much work was done by him and the adult staff and how much by the children. He told us one droll little story.

"In the beginning, we thought we could make a profit from growing strawberries, and yes, the crops were plentiful. But when we sent youngsters out into the lines of fruiting plants to harvest the strawberries, very few were in their baskets. In fact, we never made more than a few dollars from strawberry growing. Those sent to pick them ate the lot!"

"So how did you solve that problem?"

"Now we grow lemons."

Hungry children surrounded us as we walked through Santa Cruz and stopped at a street-side cafe for a lunch-time meal of burger and chips. My chair was on the pavement, and I soon noticed a boy of about ten simply staring at me as I ate. He was barefoot and dressed in a very old T-shirt and shorts, and as I finished, he crept up to me and whispered in Spanish, "Has the Senora eaten in full?"

I nodded and pushed my plate a little towards him. It still held some crumbs of meat and about four potato chips or French fries. The boy grabbed the leftovers as quickly as he could and threw them into his mouth. He knew how to eat fast, and why, because as soon as the waiter saw him, the man rushed forward brandishing a large stick and literally beat the boy away from our table. That was how many children managed to feed themselves in those days in Bolivia.

The arrogant assumptions of aid workers, however well-meaning we are in general, was brought home to me on our last day in Santa Cruz. Some representatives of an agricultural workers' union had heard we were in town and asked to see us to state their case, pleading for financial support.

We agreed to meet the reps at 10 am in the centre, and

arrived in good time from our guest house a few minutes down the road. Ten o'clock came and went, so did eleven, and we were getting impatient and slightly annoyed. Hey, we had come all the way from England, albeit on a comfortable transatlantic flight, but we could be on time, why couldn't they?

A few minutes short of noon, three weary men in cotton shirts and jeans arrived at the meeting place, just as we were preparing to give up and leave. They were very apologetic as they explained, "We set out at seven last night, after work, and have been walking all night. We had hoped to get a lift on a passing truck, but no-one came past us on the road, so we had to just keep walking. We are so happy you waited for us."

They had walked seventy kilometres. I realised then, who had made the most effort to make it to the meeting. Things are not always what they seem.

So ended my first trip to South America on behalf of Christian Aid. It gave me a drenching in the realities of how bad political leadership, especially the sort which sides all the time with the rich and powerful at the expense of the poor and marginalised, can make life so unhappy for so many people. But it also taught me that hope will spring up anywhere, like grass through concrete. It is virtually impossible to subdue the human spirit.

CHAPTER

11

Down and Out in California
1992 Back to the USA

California is a geographically diverse, warm and beautiful state of the Union, my favourite place to visit of all the parts of the USA where I have wandered, and where some of my oldest and closest friends still live. Southern California is also frenetically crazy, ruined by concrete freeways and multiple lookalike cities which resemble patchwork squares cut from very boring old shirt cloth.

Some of the city names are self-explanatory, for example "Industry," others are wildly misleading like "Lake Forest," and the roads are generally so wide you have to have a strategic plan as a pedestrian to get to the other side before the green man stops flashing.

I have returned many times, more than a dozen I'm sure over forty years, to reconnect with "family" and friends there, and my latest trip was just last summer, where I feel I deserved a medal traversing the Los Angeles basin in a hired car and flying out of Burbank Airport to connect with friends now living in Portland, Oregon.

But one of my most interesting sojourns was in January 1992, when I took a short sabbatical to see what work was being done on the ground to combat the homelessness problem. It was part of a Master's degree I was doing in Theology, so I concentrated on Church based agencies. I made some fascinating discoveries and met some reassuringly thoughtful people.

The homelessness problem had risen sharply in the late 1980s, under President Reagan's lack of interest in social programmes and concentration on tax-cutting measures to appeal to his core Republican supporters. But under his successor President George Bush, numbers of people resorting to living rough, or sleeping in the cars was even higher. How had the Churches and the Church agencies reacted?

In my home town of Whittier, the local equivalent of what the Brits would call "Churches Together," the ecumenical council, had set up a winter shelter scheme for homeless people as each church out of the local group agreed to offer temporary shelter for one night a week, through the coldest months of the year.

We visited one of these shelter schemes, and I was rather taken aback to see the Methodist Church hall (for this was the one on duty that night), was populated by whole families, including several high-school-aged children. A bed for the night and a hot meal was provided for each person accepted. Anyone on drugs or under the influence of liquor was refused entrance, and the doors were firmly closed by eight the following morning, after a light breakfast and hot drink.

The volunteer showing us round whispered, "It really is shocking. My daughter is a high-school teacher, and recognised one of her students, a very nice boy who is working hard to maintain good grades, as an overnight stayer last week, along with his family. No-one on the faculty at the school had any idea the family were homeless."

We discovered many other people in similar dire straits, due to early foreclosing of mortgages, or sudden unemployment. The received wisdom is that nearly three-quarters of American citizens are only one paycheque away from financial disaster, and I think the situation is currently very much the same in the UK.

For far too long the countries' poor wage growth, and emphasis on consumption has resulted in an explosion of personal debt, most of it on credit cards. European rates of spending on credit cards are much, much lower. This started thirty years ago, and by the 1990s was embedded in our cultures.

Debt, of course, now is woven into the warp of most people's personal financial life, with student loans pushed immediately onto a young person's back as soon as they emerge from school. If you know you will never be free of the burden, then what is another £10,000 in the scheme of things? In fact, all of the problems I witnessed up and down the state of California in 1992, are now much worse, there and in the UK. Every major city in both places now has permanent camps of homeless people, ballooning dramatically in recent times.

Running the shelters provided a temporary sticking plaster over the wounds of the homeless, but it was more than a gesture by the Churches, and, rather like child sponsorship, it provided more in value as an educational exercise for those who gave and supported the schemes, than to the overall financial emergencies faced by the recipients. Donors and volunteer helpers had a glimpse maybe, but a valuable glimpse into what life is actually like below the safety net.

In the UK, I had similar experiences around the same time, with homeless people in and around our parishes in Cheshire. The Council of Churches in Chester City were funding a soup kitchen and were chided by the rep. from one of the wealthier churches who complained, "I thought we were told that the soup kitchen would be self-supporting by now! How long are we supposed to go on providing food like this?"

My friend Sally, who managed the local men's homeless shelter in Chester, told me of similar misunderstandings. She was living temporarily with her parents in an exclusive suburb, and saw a notice advertising a residents' meeting to discuss the "undesirable elements seen in the neighbourhood."

"It was with a sudden gulp of panic," she told me, laughing, "I realised they were probably talking about me!" She generally wore black, had several piercings and a tattoo, all very daring in 1992, and obviously unsettling to those watching her get off the bus and walk home past their beautifully tended front gardens.

But back in California, I visited one church (characteristically in Oakland) which had the most vigorous social action policy of any church I have visited, anywhere. It was a United Reformed Church, a radical child of the old Presbyterian tradition, and at the time I visited, their full time Justice and Peace Minister was organising trainings for people keen to counsel and support any members of the armed forces who didn't want to fight in Iraq. Quite a few of the congregation had signed up for this training, more, I suspected, than any clients who might want to object to the war from the local army bases.

But the Church certainly showed some energy. There were more than twelve different action groups or working parties you could join, from homeless soup-runs, support for women experiencing domestic violence, book groups and meals and wheels services for "shut-ins" as the Americans call the house-bound, several youth initiatives, groups to help people suffering from various addictions, and their families and supporters. The Church also had a very active Amnesty International group, and support programmes for immigrant and un- documented people, and agricultural field workers.

The young female minister in charge of all the programmes said to me, "The Church Council are all behind the work. People know what to expect. As soon as you come through our doors, you are warmly welcomed to attend worship, but if you want to become a member of our church, then you realise that it is expected, really expected that you will join at least one working party, and commit to social reform and the alleviation of suffering. We are a working church, not a cruise ship."

I deeply admired that quite small and insignificant church, whose members were often attacked and pilloried for their stance on pacifism, anti-racism, and support for lesbian and gay people and those with HIV-AIDS. They were trying to live out the gospel of Christ, in a real, often hostile, world.

From Oakland I drove on to Sacramento, where I met a memorable group of people, managed by a vigorous Catholic Sister. Her mission was to examine all the legislation coming up before the State legislative assembly, to scrutinize it for its effect, positive or negative on the plight of the poorest people in the state.

Some people don't realise that under the American federal

political system, what goes on at national level is mirrored or echoed at the state level. There are state senators, and state representatives of the various local communities. In a state as large as California, with an economy as large as many countries, laws passed, or not passed, in Sacramento, the state capital, can have a huge effect on the lives of its residents.

The Roman Catholic nun, whose brainchild this organisation was, was a feisty, highly intelligent woman with a determination to make sure the politicians never forgot the poor. She was an advocate for the marginalised and dispossessed, emboldened by the liberal springtime which had emerged from the Catholic hierarchy after Vatican 2. I met several similar people along the way, but she was the one I remember as most clearly realising the need to grab the lawmakers by the scruff of their stiff shirt collars and force them to see the world they were creating.

I have sadly found precious few churches which live up to the proclamations of the Beatitudes, or the exhortations in Matthew, Chapter 25, Verses 34 to 46. But one of my favourites will always be All Saints Pasadena, a powerful and well attended Episcopalian Church which remains as committed to the wider gospel of social inclusion and radical action now, as it always has.

It too has multiple working groups and committees devoted to social progressive support for the most vulnerable and marginalised, and the preaching of its pastors has always been worth listening to. It's a great place and I wish we had more churches like it in the UK.

I finished my month in the USA by attending a fundraising supper for agricultural workers in Southern California and learned more of the illnesses and even deaths incurred by the harsh working conditions, the lack of shade and sufficient drinking water, and the often awful living conditions in the temporary camps for the fruit and vegetable pickers.

Nothing has changed for the better, I am sorry to say, in the thirty years since I first connected with the supporters of the programme, except that a reign of terror now rules as people are so frightened to lose their jobs and be swept up for deportation at the whim of the local ICE officers.

California's economy would literally buckle if every undocumented immigrant were to suddenly be whisked away. They provide the bulk of the farm labour and the gardening services, but also the majority of care workers for the elderly both in their homes and in all the facilities and sheltered accommodation programmes. Diversity, as well, seems to have enriched the lives of all the residents.

America is still a real melting pot, and, as I have witnessed, all the better for it. When I look back to the little isolated Kansas town, I visited back in 1971, where no-one had even seen a black man in the flesh, so to speak, I only think how sad that was, and what they must have missed out on.

The human race is funny, loving and sometimes exasperating, but people and their stories make our wonderful planet come alive, and we all need to get along much, much better. There will always be more that connects us than divides us. Don't believe anyone who tells you otherwise.

THREE

CHAPTER
12

The Land of red soil
1994 Kenya

It took many years for me to reach Africa, but it is the continent with which I have been most closely connected since the 1990s. The earth is a deep chrome red, the smell of the early morning mist rising over an African village is irresistible, and the many and various peoples are some of the most real, passionate and life-affirming human beings one will find anywhere.

The soundtrack to Africa for me has always been the earnest but cheerful chatter of little children, conversing on matters big and small. Sometimes they have been sitting on a bank, watching a river flow lazily by. Sometimes they have been clustered round the gates of a school, or outside a hut while their mother pounds manioc, with the hypnotic dull thudding sound which denotes the global reality that a woman's work is never done. Sometimes they have been playing football with a broken plastic remnant of someone else's game, sometimes hopscotch with a little stone thrown from one square to another. But there has always been chatter, laughter and conversation.

The people of Africa may not have always been blessed with easy lives or benign weather, but they certainly have the best sense of humour and the most dignity of all the people in the world. Even when they are most sad, they are always looking on the bright side. They are also the cleverest linguists in the world, moving between two, three or even four distinct languages in one conversation. I remain in awe.

My first trip to sub-Saharan Africa took place in the mid-1990s, when I spent a few weeks in Kenya. I was very excited about the trip, hosted by the Kenyan National Council of Churches, and we were accommodated in a comfortable Methodist guest house.

One of my travelling companions, a woman from North India, who ran her own agency in the UK, refused to stay there, saying it was too upmarket, and she relocated herself into central Nairobi, on a street where there was a cluster of goat-meat butchers. Unfortunately, this coincided with more than one goat-butcher family wedding, so her nights were disrupted for the rest of our stay.

Nairobi is circled by a huge outer ring of informal settlements, vast slums of hundreds of thousands of people who have mainly migrated in from the countryside in search of jobs and fortune. These places do have a vitality, but they are a cruel, almost savage environment in which to raise a family.

With Violet, a worker from the Council of Churches, we were taken to see an especially heart-breaking case. Violet was carrying a large woollen blanket, and a bagful of other supplies.

"There is a new baby," she said as we approached, "And they have very little."

The place was called, in Swahili, the word for "Rubbish." The driver dropped us off on the outskirts and we walked down alleyways running with open sewerage. It had recently rained and everywhere was drenched. We stopped at a house, which wasn't really a house, just a corrugated iron roof balanced over a small space up against a fence. The walls were made of cardboard, which was already looking sodden, and there was a piece of plastic forming some sort of door.

A worn-out looking woman of about thirty came out through the doorway and started to embrace Violet, kissing her hands. Her words, translated for us by an embarrassed Violet, were roughly, "Ah, Violet, she is our angel. She has been sent by God."

Violet handed over the blanket and dried milk. "How is the little one?" she asked?"

"Aye, aye. Not so good, and my daughter, she also has a fever."

There were several children around, so I could not quite identify where the new baby was, as this mother was thin as a rake and did not look as though she had recently given birth. Then all became sadly clear.

Lying on the one bed inside the shack there was a girl, maybe twelve years old, who was obviously not well. Violet explained she was the new baby's mother, who had been raped in their own alleyway by one of the men passing by. In fact, rape was the means by which most of the children in the vicinity had been fathered. But this little mother was no more than a child. She had been a virgin, and the pregnancy had been very hard for her. The baby had been born only two days before.

But where was the baby? It was dark in the shack and hard to see. Then on the floor I saw a little movement. I stepped back in shock, reached down and then picked up a tiny baby girl, wrapped in a tea-towel with the cord still clamped and tied up with a rag. She was no more than four pounds in weight, a tiny, fragile bundle in my two hands. Her mother was twelve and her grandmother, thirty years of age. What would her future be?

Violet arranged for medical care and promised to return later with more supplies. We left them there, the little hungry family, with no visible means of support, in a huge Nairobi slum, in a section called "Rubbish." But these people weren't rubbish. They were living, breathing miracles of creation and they deserved better.

I visited and recorded many stories, and more positive ones, over the years I have worked with Kenyan people, but none has touched my heart as much as that first encounter with the brutal reality of violence against women and girls and its inevitable outcome. As we left, the mother was still praising God for Violet, and calling her an angel, which, I agree, she most definitely was.

There was some more encouraging news at our next pastoral visit, and this story is a good example of how a little encouragement and even less money can achieve a great deal.

This story concerns a woman called Gladys, who moved into Rubbish-town, with her husband and children, hoping for a brighter future and better schools for the kids, than those available out in the rural area where they came from. Life was very tough, but they survived with her husband getting enough work as a scaffolder to bring home a little every day. However, he then fell from the top of the building where he was working, and broke his leg badly. They could only afford the most basic hospital care and he remained crippled for life, certainly unable to climb scaffolding anymore.

Things which could hardly get worse, then did. Gladys's husband confessed to her that he had a second "wife" who also had four or five children, and this wife was so badly affected by his accident that she had tried to commit suicide and was still dangerously depressed.

Gladys behaved magnificently, and took in the second wife or girlfriend, along with all her children. She now had nine children, and two other adults to feed and house, and she was the only adult breadwinner. On top of this, her eldest son, who was fifteen, had started to go off the rails, partly because he was disgusted by his father. He was running with a gang of pickpockets and drug-dealers through the city, and had dropped out of school.

Gladys had finally admitted to defeat, and had turned to Violet. What on earth could she do now?

We met her in the local marketplace by her stall, and she explained. Firstly, Violet had lifted her up and encouraged her not to give up hope of a better future. Violet had made her feel that she had a good friend, who had belief in her. Along with this came a small cash grant, £5 or $8, so she could set up in business.

Gladys took the money and bought a 25lb sack of corn with it. This she divided up into 1lb portions, re-bagging them and selling them each for twice what she'd paid wholesale. Local families could only afford a few shillings at a time, so quickly bought out her stock. So she now had £10. She bought another sack and a half and used the remaining cash to feed her family and pay the rent.

This is how, over the course of six months, she had secured her family's future, and saved their lives. Now her husband sat at home, bagging up maize, and yam flour for her, while she ran the stall. The co-wife cared for the children and cooked supper for them all, no longer suicidal.

What about the troublesome son? Well, she had sent him back to the village to live with his grandparents. Away from the gangs, he was a different boy, and was once again doing well in the local school.

This is a short story about good news, about how a little can go a long way, and how the most important thing some people need to survive is simply friendship and encouragement. It cheered me up in my first few days in Kenya, but I still remembered the little new-born baby, and her slim chance of survival. If she is alive today, she will be twenty-four years old, most probably with children of her own. I do hope she has had a better life than her mother and grandmother.

The connections between ordinary people round the world never receive the publicity or the resourcing which the rich and powerful have. But I have seen the magnetism between people, and the immense good done by charities who collect money, dollar by dollar, from small collections, individual donors, church appeals, sponsored walks and the like. The people who raised money in the UK by running a bake-sale or putting a little aside each month, they are the ones who enabled Violet to do her work in Kenya, or the small grant made to Gladys. They paid for the literacy classes in Bolivia, and the Young Christian Workers in the Philippines.

I don't want to state the obvious too much, and there are

certainly a lot of false prophets and charlatans out there who will rook the poor widow of her pension in the name of their particular brand of Christianity. But a gift of money to the most reputable aid agencies will cause rivers to flow through the desert, and the dry lands turned into a swamp, as it said in the Book of Isaiah.

Sceptics often claim the money doesn't get through to the poorest. But it does. And if there is fraud, or corruption, whether in London or Lusaka, New York or Nairobi, then the obvious answer, as one elderly lady said to me once, is "We must just give more. We still have so much surplus; our own survival will never be in doubt."

We later had a day trip out of Nairobi, about seventy miles towards the east coast. The landscape was very dry in that region, white and sandy everywhere, and the spasmodic flashes of green stood out like little oases. They were mainly, lines of trees growing into the banks of rivers and indicating where precious flowing water might be found.

Our destination was a village high up on a steep hill, where people had been awarded a grant to improve their village hall. Meeting places are surprisingly difficult to find in rural Africa for clubs and self-improvement societies. Most gatherings, even funerals and weddings, are held outside, as people's homes are always far too small to accommodate more than the immediate family. A community centre, or village hall is a huge asset, and it was soon booked up every day of the week.

The National Council of Churches lent us a large four-by-four vehicle, probably a Toyota land cruiser, which are everywhere the international aid workers go.

On this day in Kenya, the sun was beating hot and we

were glad of the air-conditioning afforded by the vehicle. We turned off the main road to the coast and started to climb. After a mile or so we passed two young girls, carrying the ubiquitous water containers, fully loaded with several gallons of water.

These are so heavy, even I find them hard to lift. The usual method is to twist a cloth round and round one's head to provide a better grip and then hoist the heavy bottle or bucket above. If you balance it carefully and keep your neck in a certain position you can carry water for far longer than if you struggle with it on your back.

I remember thinking how graceful, even elegant, these girls looked. They stepped back from the track to let our vehicle pass and waved in a friendly way. I hoped they didn't have far to go, as the watercourse was already a few hundred yards behind us.

We travelled on in a cloud of dust, bumping over the unmade road and swerving round boulders, until we finally ascended the last bend and found ourselves safely at our destination, maybe three miles further on, high up in the hills.

When we jumped out, the village women immediately began to sing, welcoming us to their place, and ushering us in. They offered us water and soap to wash our dusty hands, and led us to the feast they had prepared, for we were already late for lunch.

An hour later, we had consumed the chicken and rice, and Ugale meal, and were now being offered fried balls made with dried milk and white flour, which were quite a luxury item for dessert. The sun had slipped from being directly over our heads, and was going west.

Then there was a slight noise at the edge of the crowd. The

two girls we had passed so casually four miles back down the hill had just arrived, with the four gallons of water. They had carried it uncomplaining and still smiling at the end of their three-hour climb, through the hottest part of the day, on their young heads, so that we could have a cup of tea.

"Do you take sugar?" their mother asked us.

Green Beans

One of the memorable trips on that first visit to Kenya, was on a warm and dusty Sunday, when we were invited to visit another rural agricultural project, which was improving the soil so the subsidence farmers could increase their crop yield. They had no heavy equipment, not even an ox or two to plough the heavy red soil.

"It is very tedious, being a subsistence farmer," sighed one man to me. He and his wife and children toiled for hours every day to grow crops for their own food, and to sell to the export firm which had swept into their valley. The best land had long been taken by European coffee plantation owners, but this new multi-national company promised a fresh deal.

"We've been promised good money though for green beans, if we can produce them to the standard needed in your supermarkets. But there is little margin in it for us."

I asked him to explain further. Well, he was contracted to buy the seeds, chemical fertiliser and all the packing boxes from the company, at the price they dictated. He was to provide the land, all the labour, and the local agricultural expertise to grow the French beans, as well as the water, which in itself was a great challenge.

He showed me the beans he and his family had picked and

packed into cardboard boxes piled high inside their tiny home. His children ran about barefooted and dressed in hardly more than rags. They looked underweight, and none seemed to be in school.

"How much do you make per kilogram?"

He said it was about 12 pence, but after all the overheads were taken into consideration, the profit per kilo was about 6-8 pence. I recognised the name on the boxes of beans. When I returned to the UK, I went into the supermarket which sold those very beans and looked at the pricing. As consumers, one would pay 60 pence for 100 grams. Or £6 a kilo. Quite a mark-up, eh?

No wonder the multi-national food giants think it is worthwhile taking a flight out to Kenya. International trade is all very well, but not based on the labour of young children whose parents cannot afford schooling or shoes for them.

This story is sadly repeated everywhere I have travelled, whether it concerns cocoa pod growers in Ghana, or flowers for the North American Valentine's Day market, grown in sweat-shop conditions in Colombia. From the gold miners and pineapple growers of the Philippines, to the bean farmers of Kenya, the poor are supporting the lifestyle of the rich and powerful in a ridiculously unjust way.

Why is there not more outrage? It takes a full belly to give one the strength and the appetite for the struggle. But one suspects that one day there is bound to be a fightback. This current system is so unbalanced as to be unsustainable. Maybe the single-use plastic used to wrap the out-of-season African "French" beans will soon choke the world's oceans, and people will realise their mistake.

Drumming for God

We'd been invited to a Church service and a meal to celebrate the new soil improvement project, and we were running late. In fact, we were two hours late. I was convinced the service would be long finished by the time our battered vehicle was finally winding its way to the Church, somewhere in North Central Kenya.

We had stopped to cross over a flooded river where the bridge had been knocked away. Kenya seemed either to be all parched and dried up, or flooded. The locals had come out of the bush from no-where and had made a temporary bridge with brushwood and some planks. It looked nothing if not terrifying, but my motto wherever I travelled across the world was "Let the Driver drive."

These mainly young men were magicians when it came to getting their vehicles round, over or through the most impossible terrain. They could fix most things on the road as well, and if they couldn't, would either go themselves, or send a young brother running back a few miles to find someone who could. Locals dropped twists of grass on the road before and after a breakdown to warn any travellers coming behind that there might be trouble ahead.

Driving with my host, Mary, a senior worker at the Council of Churches, I remarked that in England people often left flowers beside the road, at places where their loved ones had died in an accident.

"Oh, we couldn't do that here, "she laughed ruefully. "There would be so many, the entire road would be blocked."

Her biggest fear, though, was of being "car-napped" and held for ransom. Anyone in a vehicle was seen as super-rich and therefore fair game. We never travelled after dark, certainly. Mary did herself get car-napped a few years later, but managed, thankfully to negotiate her way to safety.

One terrible accident had already happened on the main road into Nairobi, a month or two before I arrived. A truck full of policemen and cadets, on their way to march in the Presidential parade had overturned on the road when a tyre blew out.

The truck was packed full of standing officers, and most were killed. It wasn't the road traffic accident which actually caused such a high death-toll, but the poor truck maintenance and the extreme danger of their own weapons. There had been strict instructions from the Government officials that they were to be fully dressed in their uniforms with fixed bayonets on their rifles as they set out from their training camp, ready to march out smartly and salute their president.

On this occasion, we walked apologetically into a packed Church belonging to the Independent Church of Kenya, a local denomination which had a model of Mount Kenya actually carved into the central altar. The assembly stopped praising God and turned to welcome us enthusiastically, including a front row of elderly men with white hair and walking sticks.

"You're not late at all, we have hardly started. We have just had the first sermon from our deacon," said one of the welcome team. "It has been one for the men, on the dangers of imbibing too much beer."

The service had started at 10 am. It was now noon, and it finished sometime after 2.00pm. The elderly men at the front, we were told, were the honoured veterans of the Mau-Mau rising back in the 1950s. They had been tortured and imprisoned by the British for seeking independence and rising up against the Crown. Here, in this small rural community, they were still revered and held in the highest esteem.

After the service, I engaged a delightful old lady in conversation who had played an enormous drum accompanying all the many hymns and worship songs. She was very skilled and her playing took one back into the Africa of many years before.

"I have played the drum all my life," she told me, "since I was six. And my mother played it for worship before me."

I calculated that she must be well into her eighties, and this was 1994. So, she must have been playing for worship before the Christian missionaries had even set up churches in this part of Kenya.

I asked her about this, and she replied, "Oh of course we worshipped God before the missionaries came, but in our own way. We just let them share the story of Jesus with us, and then carried on. It is the easiest thing in the world to be a missionary in Africa. Just put up a notice on a tree, and crowds of people will join you there in prayer. We are a very spiritual people!"

Some days later my Indian friend and I were somehow separated from the rest of our party. We were north of Meru, beyond Mount Kenya and somewhere on the way to the Somalian border, and had now hitched a ride in a Mother's Union pickup truck. A young Anglican clergyman was our host for this section of our visit, and he spoke nostalgically about his years studying for the ministry at Trinity College, Bristol.

"It was hard to leave," he freely confessed. "My fellow ordinands didn't really understand what I would come back to. Being a Christian minister here is not like it is in the

UK, because we're not supported financially; our parishioners cannot afford to keep their own families, let alone ours. When my prospective father-in-law heard I wanted to be a minister he was furious. 'You realise you are condemning my daughter to a life of miserable poverty,' he said, 'and my grandchildren will go hungry and without shoes.'"

Worse than this, though was the danger this young clergyman lived with every day of his life, ferrying food aid and other relief north to the Sudanese and Somalian refugee camps at the northern-most point of his parish, a parish larger than the whole of Yorkshire.

His wife said to us, "Whenever he leaves on another trip, we say goodbye as though we may never meet again, because that could easily be the outcome. More than one of his fellow pastors have been shot on the road north."

Because there was heavy flooding in the area, and the road out was impassable, the Vicar suggested we stay overnight in a nearby truckers' stop. He could not accommodate us, as the vicarage had no furniture or beds. He took us to the inn he knew, where they found us a double room away from the bar area, and separate from the dormitories where the male drivers bunked down. Everyone was friendly, and we were assured that if we took a Coca-Cola and sat in the garden, supper could be provided in the time it would take to cook it.

"What's on the menu?" asked my friend, of the young man who served us.

"Ah, chicken and chips, or goat and chips."

Being Indian, and enduring a week in the alleyway of the goat butchers, she thought she might take revenge.

"Goat sounds good. I haven't had goat for years."

"A thousand apologies, but the goat is off."

"Oh well then, chicken and chips," she said and I nodded in agreement.

We had just settled to enjoying our coke when an almighty screaming could be heard from behind the kitchen yard. A cockerel was having its neck pulled.

"I'm glad I didn't insist on the goat," whispered my friend.

Thirty minutes later, though, a plate of chicken and French fries was set before us, along with tomato ketchup. Fast food, African style. I'm afraid we tucked in, and it was very good. The cockerel enjoyed his life until the very moment he lost it, less than an hour before we, and several other people, ate him.

CHAPTER
13

On the Shores of Lake Victoria
2008-16 Western Kenya and Uganda

It is a beautiful lake straddling the shores of three huge countries, Kenya, Uganda and Tanzania, but Lake Victoria, named after the British Queen, provides an attractive view to some of the poorest people in Africa. The islands which are scattered across it also provide a haven for the most marginalised and most dispossessed of humans, including sex workers shunned by their own clients because they carried HIV, albino young people, of whom there are a surprising number in East Africa, and the generally despised and rejected. On top of those people there are simply a general population too poor to live anywhere else. The water also carries a parasite which can kill you. This has somewhat depressed the tourist trade in the region, to put it mildly.

It was 2015 when my elder son and I visited Homa Bay, on the Kenyan side of the Lake, in what should have been a very pleasant area, with productive farmland and relatively good rainfall. Yet it was home to people made wretched by the extraordinary high level of HIV, and because the provision of effective medicines wasn't sufficient, a subsequently very high death-toll of its young people from complications due to full-blown Aids.

One such woman, Muriel, who was in her early thirties, lay on a pallet in her mother's tumbledown farmhouse. She was as fragile and as thin as a gazelle, with huge eyes in a face wasted by pain and the constant coughing of the TB which had crept into her body through the AIDS virus.

Our associates had brought fruits and good quality vegetables which she was supposed to have on a daily basis, but the family could not afford. Her mother was caring for six orphaned grandchildren already, and soon Muriel's daughter would be added to the permanent household. Muriel had been given the HIV virus by her husband who had since left to seek work in Tanzania, and she died just three days after our visit, while we were still in town.

The Bicycle

One of the worst side effects of the HIV pandemic in the area came from a myth that sex with a virgin would cure it in a man. This is one true story of what happened to a little girl as a result.

Ten-year-old Victoria was Muriel's niece, living with her grandmother and cousins after her parents had both died. One evening she was given a few shillings and sent to buy bread, a route which took her through some rough ground and then the alleyways of their slum quadrant of the city.

Night fell and the child had not returned so her grandmother began to be seriously worried. She set off down through the high reeds towards the lake, calling all the time, and also joined by a neighbour or two.

Hours later, they found Victoria, bleeding from her vagina and soaking wet, cowering in the bushes close to the shores of the lake. She had been raped and beaten, and had tried to drown herself in the Lake, but couldn't manage to finish what her attacker had started.

There was no money to pay for transport, but her grandmother managed somehow to get Victoria up to the medical clinic at the top of the town, where her injuries had to be stitched up, and she was given antibiotics. Subsequent blood tests showed that she had been infected with HIV by the rapist. He was known to the family, but escaped before the police arrested him and disappeared off to Nairobi.

Victoria was by no means the youngest child raped in this way and for this reason. Even baby girls were not safe. But she suffered greatly. She became stigmatised herself and stopped going to school where she was bullied.

While I was there, we were able to find her a local boarding school, with a sympathetic headmistress. My son felt so sorry for her, he asked her grandmother what might cheer her up.

"A red bicycle," was the answer, so that was arranged, not red, but silver, and the last memory I have of her is riding her bicycle with her cousins up and down the tracks by their tumble-down little farm. She would have to be on anti-viral medicines for the rest of her life.

Samuel the Sandal maker

A young man named Sam sat by the roadside in Homa Bay city making sandals from old car tyres. He would draw round your foot and cut the rubber with a knife, then construct the sandal.

His own feet were pretty useless, one of them bearing an enormous tumour which made his leg swell up like an elephant's. This gave him constant agony, and the only medical solution would be surgery to amputate his leg below the knee.

Sam was literally between a rock and a very hard place. Not only could he not afford the expensive operation, but as a one-legged single man without any money for a decent prosthetic leg, his prospects were minimal. So, he sat by the roadside making sandals for those fortunate people who walked back and forth on two good legs in front of his pitch.

Sam was part of a table-top banking group I was visiting, which literally had the power by some financial magic to make money from nothing, or at least from tiny amounts of coins.

It worked like this. There were ten in the group, with an elected chair and secretary and treasurer. For the sake of argument, let's say each person brought £1 to the monthly meeting. So, in January £10 was on the table. By contributing, each member then had the right, one at the time, to borrow the £10 for a month, at 10%. People applied to be the borrower for the month.

So, having used the money to set up some tiny enterprise, or for some need, the borrower would return next month with £11. The £1 was set aside, and the £10 lent out again, along with another £10 brought by the members to the next meeting. Sometimes the money on the table was split into halves or even a third, but the lending time was usually just one month.

By the middle of the year there would be £60 plus the added interest, circulating round the members. Within a year, as much as £150 would be available to be loaned out, and that sort of money could set up a workshop or pay for building materials to build a tiny house. At the end of the year, the money raised in interest was divided and shared out round the group as a Christmas dividend. It was a successful scheme and helped many of the group start or improve their businesses. Sam was one, and I hope he survived.

I stayed for two weeks in the town of Homa Bay, and tried to provide some practical suggestions for improving the chances for the local agency to become self-sufficient, and to reform its own governance, but it was one of my least successful interventions in other people's business.

There was a power struggle going on within the organisation, which I, and my son, who was working with me on the commission, had no tools to solve, and ultimately the main losers were the local community members, struggling so hard to survive the immense public health crisis of the prevalence of HIV. This overwhelmed the resources of the district healthcare professionals, and sliced through the young adult population like a demonic scythe.

Girls' education remains the most powerful tool, in my opinion, in fighting poverty in Africa. If a girl can stay in school through puberty and not drop out at twelve or thirteen, she will be spared the usual trap of early marriage, and the assault on her health and independence of the four or five babies she will bear before the age eighteen. But staying in school presents a much harder challenge to young girls across the world than it might do in North America or Europe.

I connected with other organisations in the Homa Bay area, all working for change, and one of the most impressive was providing a mentoring service for schoolgirls struggling to complete their secondary school education. There were definite reasons why comparatively few girls transitioned successfully from primary to secondary school in the district.

Unlike their male counterparts, who grew stronger and more independent in adolescence, the girls became handicapped in a dramatic way once they reached puberty and started their periods. It was in Western Kenya also, that I first became first aware of why "being on the rag," did indeed justify the tag it had gained many years earlier, "the Curse."

To start with, there were no decent toilets at the school for students, and no privacy for girl students where they could change their pads, or dispose of soiled towels. This meant that, in practice, most girls just stayed at home for the length of their period, meaning they regularly lost one week out of four of their education.

At secondary school level, there were far more male than female teachers, and these men, I was told, showed scant respect or understanding to girls who needed this time off, or who were taken ill in class. The traditional "solution" to girls' menstrual cycles, early marriage as soon as menses started, would automatically mean an end to any educational opportunity.

The next barrier of course, to girls who resisted being pulled into marriage, often to men older than their own fathers, was of course, sexual assault. One application for funding which I evaluated, was for a scheme to provide bicycles for girls to use to travel to and from school.

When I queried the need for these, it was explained that in this way, the girls, by pedalling furiously, might escape all the youths and young men who would regularly accost them in the bushes along the road from the school back down into the villages surrounding the school!

Even bicycles couldn't help the female students of one school I visited. I once worked with a project in Kenya to protect girls from sexual attacks. Many secondary school girls, without any sanitary provision, or even secure toilets, would stay home one week in four while they were on their period, as there was nowhere, they could change a pad or even find a sanitary pad in their schools. Of course, they fell behind the boys and did less well in the national tests.

Even worse, something which really shocked me, was that their biggest fear was of the School Principal, who in their community held a sort of sleazy Droit du Seigneur over his teenage female pupils and routinely raped them himself, in his office. No wonder few of the bright little girls who passed out of primary school aged twelve, survived to go onto to college at eighteen.

The "Me Too" movement has revealed the extent to which such sexual bullying has pervaded even the dreamland of Hollywood, and it certainly happens wherever there is that power imbalance between the sexes, (in other words, everywhere in the world!) but the success of girls in Kenya and other African countries who have emerged as highly qualified, articulate and courageous young women is only to be applauded the louder. None of them will have had an easy ride, even with a new bicycle.

Across the silver waters of Lake Victoria lies Uganda, a country especially dear to my heart. Northern Uganda is a strange place of extreme contrasts. Water is carried for miles in the dry season, and yet whole landscapes are flooded after the rains which feed the tributaries of the River Nile, taking the water north.

The subsistence farmers struggle to grow enough to feed themselves and their children, more often women struggle by hand to farm a five acre plot of heavy red soil, but the herders of the great cattle with their impressive horns wander the bush, clashing with them as the cattle invade the farmer's field to eat the crops and search for the scant water. Tribal loyalties are all important, and there is often a feud going on between the various people, the farmers like the Teso, and the Karamojong, the now sadly coralled nomadic people of the cattle herding tradition.

About twelve years ago, I was part of a well-intentioned intervention to try to bring reconciliation between these sworn enemies by setting up a "peace" camp in between them, with brave individuals from each community pledging to live together, sharing a life of prayer and Christian worship while trying to help set up small scale development projects.

My one visit to the region did not help the local conflict in any meaningful way, but it taught me many things. One was the fury and tenacity of people to hang onto their dignity and pride under all circumstances, even when they are reduced to living without their land or their livestock.

One day, a lean, very tall, village chief of the Karamojong walked into our camp. There was a back story to his visit. A year or two before, the Ugandan government had stripped the Karamojong of their right to own cattle, and in doing so, reduced them to immediate destitution. This was supposed to be the answer to the constant rustling and conflict between various cattle herders, but there were other more profound political forces at play.

Every day we could see the giant trucks on the main road up to the city of Moroto and beyond, coming back with massive hauls of quarried stones to build the presidential palaces for the heads of the country and their friends. The very land on which the Karamojong stood was being ripped out from under them. Local opposition was stifled, and there was very little recompense in any tangible way for the exploitation of the land in terms of water, electricity, or decent side roads to various communities.

The elderly chief had come to the camp for some food relief for his starving people. What could he do? The answer seemed to him to be both degrading and ludicrous.

"Have you ever thought of keeping rabbits?"

He had spat on the ground and disappeared back into the savage landscape of his homeland.

But while we were there, a year later, he had returned. Animals were animals, and he was a stockman. If he couldn't breed cattle, then maybe he could start again with rabbits.

"What would it cost?" he asked, "And how would I go about it?"

The old chief's ability to endure, and ultimately adapt is maybe one reason why the human spirit still burns brightly over the plains and hills of Northern Uganda, which have seen so much conflict, and, as a result, have to house so many refugees and internally displaced people.

Another story, not a direct parallel, but an interesting one, was told to me when my husband was Priest in Charge of churches on the estate of the Duke of Devonshire in Derbyshire. This meant that we lived next door to the Dowager Duchess, youngest sister of the Mitford clan. She did not share all their notoriety but had the same ability to tell a good story. I also heard it from the stockman himself, still then very fit and active in his nineties.

In the 1960s, the writing was on the wall – the renowned Chatsworth stud, which for more than a century had bred the giant farm horses to work the land, was finally completely redundant. Tractors had replaced the great Shire horses, and it was decided for economic reasons to close the breeding programme and slaughter all the stallions and remaining mares.

The stockman in charge was completely devastated. Caring for these wonderful animals had been his life work, since joining the estate as a young boy straight out of the army. But it happened, and he was sunk into a huge depression.

However, the new Duchess shared his love of horses, and offered him a fresh beginning. How about breeding Shetland ponies? To begin with, he walked away, disgusted. To go from twenty-hand horses, down to miniature horses of six or seven? It was an insult. But he thought things over, swallowed his pride and asked her exactly what she had in mind. So started a new beginning. Together they built up one of the best studs of Shetlands anywhere in the world, and their offspring won prizes across Britain. A horse was still a horse, after all.

In Europe we have no idea of the numbers of refugees which African countries willingly absorb from neighbouring conflicts. I met a young Sudanese boy who had been a refugee for ten years, since he was six. Wandering across the thousands of miles of the great continent, he had learned several different languages, which he spoke fluently, including English.

His schooling had been measured in months rather than years, but he was now relatively stable in Kenya and in school. He was registered with the UN refugee services, and his heart's desire was to reach Canada, where he vaguely remembered he had an uncle. He lived day to day, in what he stood up in, but he devoured knowledge, friendship with strangers, and breathed in the oxygen of hope.

When I read almost daily of the thousands of young people desperate to find somewhere to live and start a new life, I often think of him and hope he was not one of the many so casually left to endure the horrible death by drowning in the Mediterranean.

I had a closer link with a young Ugandan girl called Sally, and her story is a salutary one. Sally and her younger brother Gus had been orphaned when their parents both died of Aids. They were in the notional care of their young aunt, who could not afford to support them. I was teaching at the time in a UK college, and one of my students came to me in tears. She had asked for sponsors for her friend's niece and nephew at the Church she attended and had been initially well received.

Joyous, she had written to her friend in Uganda, who had enrolled Sally and Gus into school on the back of this promise of sponsorship. But now the church people in England had given 'back word' and reconsidered their offer of long-term support.

"Oh, for goodness sake!" I thought, and felt the honour of British Christian decency rested on my desk. "Tell your friend not to worry, I'll take on the school sponsorship." And so, began a twenty-year commitment of friendship to Sally.

Her brother Gus dropped out, failed his exams, and did not do well, but Sally struggled through to her school certificate and then went on to a catering college, still supported by regular payments I sent through a missionary society where her aunt worked.

Something slipped though. The aunt had four children of her own, and their whole mission depended on donor support from the UK and the USA. After Sally's first year in college, she decided the money I was sending was better used caring for her own children, and told her niece I had stopped contributing. Sally had to drop out of college and find low-paid work as an unqualified cleaner in a big hotel. Neither she nor I knew about this until a few years later, when I was in Kampala and decided to look her up.

But Sally's real adventures, if you can call them that, came later. We had kept in touch and I had sent her the money to start a small shop selling electrical goods. She didn't seem to be making much progress, and I asked to see her management accounts. Then she confessed she had used the money to join an agency which was going to send her to a Gulf state to work there. She was just waiting for confirmation, and the date of her flight.

I rolled my eyes, and sent several warning emails about the dangers such a journey might entail for her, physically, financially and also in terms of trafficking. But Sally assured me all would be well; it was a reputable Ugandan agency and lots of other young women were taking the same route out of poverty.

Nine months later, the inevitable tale of woe turned up in my inbox. She was working long hours in a supermarket in Doha, but, four months earlier, the boss had suddenly stopped paying the girls. He said their agent in Kampala had not repaid him for his investment in paying their airfares. The money she had already paid this agent had been swallowed up, and she and her friend would have to work for nothing to pay off the debt.

After four months she was penniless, hungry, and her shoes had worn out. It was the little detail of the shoes which moved me, it was so classic. She had gone to the Ugandan consulate but they said nothing could be done. Her employer held her passport and she would not be allowed to leave without his permission. She was essentially enslaved. It is too long a tale to explain exactly how I managed to help Sally escape and get back to Uganda, but she was lucky to have me as her only solvent friend. Many like her are still trafficked and trapped across the world.

Like the Philippines twenty years earlier, a country like Uganda producing bright, hardworking young people, regularly exports them as collateral in the global rigged system of the powerful against the poor. Sally now works in Saudi Arabia, cleaning other people's houses, but at least she is not abused or exploited illegally, for now anyway.

I met many resourceful and unselfish people in Uganda, and working with Ugandan expat people in the UK. The current Archbishop of York, John Sentamu, and his wife Margaret were friends of ours when they first came to Cambridge escaping Idi Amin's brutal regime, and I was delighted when I first visited their home country. Our paths parted as he progressed through the ranks of the Church of England and we have not kept in touch, but I always remember John saying every shirt he ever had as a boy had been worn by all his older brothers before him.

In the north, a local worker told me that in one Karamojong village there was just one dress deemed respectable enough to go to the town, and whichever woman needed it could wear it. Bras were an unheard-of luxury. The strength of Ugandan women was brought home to me on my last day in that camp.

We saw two extra people sitting by the open-air kitchen range, being given water by the cook. Who were they? Two woman who had walked from a named place far to the north, in search of grain to plant and grow for their families.

How far was this place? More than a hundred miles, and they had walked all the way. They would walk home again, as well, in a day or two, if they could find the seeds and other supplies they needed, carrying them on their backs.

CHAPTER

14

The Effects of War
2002-08 Sierra Leone

For five years, between 2003 and 2008, I held the post of Executive Director of an effective small charity based in Bakewell, Derbyshire. It was called Village Aid, and, during the time I was in post, it grew in its capacity to help communities in West Africa, and in its ability to engage with young people in the Derbyshire and Staffordshire Peak district, to teach them about conflict resolution and development.

The latter was through the medium of educational drama and role play, with a gifted teacher. It was a productive and stimulating time for us all, and my post also gave me the chance to travel extensively along the back roads of Ghana, The Gambia, Cameroon and Sierra Leone.

In fact, it was a trip to Sierra Leone in 2002 which had prompted me to switch careers back into development work from a six-year stint in education. In 2002 I went there as a lecturer in spirituality, joining a leadership-training programme to refresh the war-weary ministers and other church leaders, both ordained and lay, in Sierra Leone.

For most of the previous decade they had existed on a starvation diet of survival in the midst of conflict, without any in-service training or resources. Many of them had been made homeless, their parish houses and manses destroyed, along with their small libraries of bibles and textbooks. Some had fled the country when and if they could join family members overseas, some survived in displaced persons camps, whilst others struggled on in ministry, struggling to keep up the morale of terrified and impoverished congregations.

I have avoided naming names, and citing many organisations in this book, but here I would like to highlight the work of Revd Richard Jackson, a Methodist minister whose vision made an important contribution to lifting the morale of so many Christian ministers in Sierra Leone. In subsequent years, Richard and his volunteer teams have progressed to running excellent diploma and certificate courses for practising church people in several other African countries. This work in 2002 was very special, because it brought light into a situation which shocked me to the core, even though I had witnessed some of the direst poverty on the planet.

Richard, a colleague at Cliff College, was also effective in persuading publishers and charities specialising like SPCK and the Evangelical Literature Trust, to provide at give-away prices a new personal library for each of the 100 plus people who attended the lectures and undertook to study for the Diploma. These resources were delivered in Sierra Leone through the Methodist Church in Ireland's Container Ministry. The full story of this partnership in training programme can be found in the published book 'Going and Growing' authored by Richard Jackson. As a result, each person took dozens of modern textbooks, bible study guides and course notes home with them.

In 2002, Sierra Leone was like a patient in the recovery room after a major road traffic accident, but its broken and bruised society was not caused by chance, but by a bitter civil war that spilled over from Liberia. Now is not the place, and I do not have the expertise, to unpack everything which caused the civil war, but I saw its results, and they made me draw a deep breath of horror.

Sierra Leone, forty years before, had been a progressive beacon of light in West Africa. Its University was renowned, its children had one of the highest rates of literacy in the continent. Its healthcare was boosted by the existence of some excellently equipped hospitals.

All of this had been torn apart by ten years of conflict. As I walked round the ruins of Nixon Memorial Hospital in up-country Segbwema in the Eastern Province, and saw its destroyed buildings, the ruins of its X-ray equipment, the broken windows and smashed up furniture, I could only think of the human misery caused to so many by the annihilation of medical provision.

In 2002, I was told that only one single paediatric surgeon remained in post in Freetown, and he was a very elderly man, whose hands shook as he applied a scalpel to his young patients. Someone who acted as his theatre nurse told me this.

The situation was of course made worse by the number of young amputees struggling to survive. Hacking off arms and legs was not invented by Africans of course. The worst atrocities ever were committed by the regime in the lands now known as the Democratic Republic of Congo, and Congo-Brazzaville in the nineteenth century, as a brutal incentive for the native population to produce more rubber for the Belgian colonists. Amputation in Sierra Leone became the 'rebels' most effective means of terrorising and neutralising any opposition. A sharp machete and total disregard for human life sent a terrifying message to those who tried to defend their homes and livelihood.

Freetown suffered many attacks by roving rebel groups. Many of its central landmark buildings had been damaged. The political and social infrastructure was struggling to maintain some control of the capital city, as well as to provide some protection to outlying communities. The streets were overcrowded with unemployed young people and other casualties of the conflict, many of them amputees. They were mostly trying to pick themselves up by their own bootstraps. The problem was, none of them had boots, and some didn't have the correct number of feet.

Children were everywhere, selling shirts and bags, and sunglasses if they were in their teens. Younger children tried to sell paper tissues, small bags of water, chewing gum, old comics. It was a population of hungry children, and I very rarely saw a head of grey hair. I would watch the throngs of young men pacing the streets, walking everywhere, and think to myself: every one of these boys needs a meal today; everyone needs somewhere to sleep; how will they find such things?

However, the older population of Freetown, in particular, clung on to the old ways, the old courtesies. Church life was central to most people's weekly routine, and the churches I was taken to, as part of my first trip, echoed with all the old traditions from Victorian England and very formal they were too. I visited one church, where a fully robed choir in cassocks and surplices sang "Zadok the Priest" in the service in 95 degrees Fahrenheit. They sang it beautifully too, accompanied by a sixteen-year-old organist producing magical sounds out of a wheezing and groaning organ.

"Why have you chosen that anthem?" I asked at the end, as I congratulated them. The answer contained a far-from-small reproach at my ignorance.

"Because it is the Queen's Golden Jubilee of course!"

Another incident in another service reminded me of the power of the mobile phone, which had just become the go-to accessory for the Sierra Leone man about town. It was a large Church, with a large congregation. We were about to have our fifth collection or whip-round of the service. (A tip if you ever visit a Church in Sierra Leone: divide your intended collection into at least seven portions, as the buckets come round regularly, not just once!)

I was caught out by a "Birthday" collection which ran like this. "Come out brothers and sisters and give joyfully to the Lord if your birthday was on a Monday!"

And so, it went on. I felt secure, clutching my few remaining Leones, as I had no idea what day of the week I was born on. But the minister was wise to that ruse. His final appeal was "Come out all you folks who cannot remember which day of the week you were born on!" So, we were all caught.

It was a jovial and merry way of extracting funds, and not too misused. The Churches I visited, unlike the planted denominations from the new world, were chronically poor.

But people liked to put on a good show, and dressed immaculately for Church, with hats and gloves and the women usually wore stockings, regardless of the heat. I was permanently the worst dressed of the women in any gathering, so much so that people often assumed I must be some kind of nun, and often called me Sister.

At the same service the Minister ascended the pulpit to preach, resplendent in his canonical garb, and began a long sermon delivered in Krio, (a kind of Pidgin English, developed by the Creole people, largely descendants of released slaves from many parts of Africa). This Krio language is used by the sixteen different tribes alongside their own language group within the country, a nation-state which, is only the size of Wales. After about ten minutes, the minister's mobile phone rang.

In those days, this was quite a novelty, and the whole congregation shared a frisson of excitement.

"Excuse me," he said, and fumbled under all his garments to retrieve the phone from his pocket. Then I was astonished as, instead of quickly checking the caller's identity and closing the phone, or even connecting up and telling the person he would call back later, he proceeded to have a long and rambling conversation, about not very much as far as I could gather. One more indication, though of how important 'people contact' is to the African. All two hundred or so of us listened along until he finally hung up. He then resumed haranguing his folk on the dangers of hard liquor.

There were more than fifty children present at the service, but they were invisible and inaudible, sitting as quietly as little mice, until they were finally invited to the front to receive a blessing, when a host of tiny heads, the girls' hair braided beautifully and adorned with little plastic hair beads and other ornaments emerged from the pews. I was in awe.

The trip to Sierra Leone in 2002 changed the course of my life, as previous pivotal events, recounted in earlier chapters had also done. I decided to seek an opening through which I could be involved in hands-on work with rural African communities, the ones so often forgotten by the large agencies, and I found it within Village Aid.

I went back to Sierra Leone twice in the next five years, and heard and saw many more living stories of its pain, and of its remodelling. I have also made many friends in the UK from Sierra Leone, and can testify to their sterling characters and endurance. It is a country, rather like the USA in some ways, in that everyone who settled there in the 1800s had lost their original culture, and could not quite identify from where their family had originally come.

For a people so bound up in their culture and the veneration of ancestors, this was maybe the most ruthless rape of identity connected with the three-hundred-year slave trade. The people kidnapped into slavery had their history, even their names and their languages ripped from them, so when they settled in Sierra Leone and Liberia, as free people, it was something they were forced to reconstruct, and it is still very much a work in progress.

DNA availability is, of course, transforming this, and also revealing how inter-connected the whole world is. I have a friend from Cameroon, from the Fula population of semi nomadic cattle-herding tradition, found also in Sierra Leone, who discovered his DNA contained European traces.

Essentially what all my travels have taught me is the simple truth that human beings are pretty much all the same and share the same basic range of needs, emotional responses and talents, though some are more developed by culture than others. What makes us happy doesn't vary very much: personal relationships and close friendships, good enough health so we are not in constant pain, and the belief that we matter, that our contribution to the world is valued. All this is universal.

One of the most attractive aspects of Muslim public prayer is the sight of all men together kneeling and placing their foreheads to the floor before God, regardless of rank. I know inclusivity ends there, and women cannot even join in with the group, but to see a hundred men, rich and powerful next to penniless and marginalised, all kneeling as one, this sends out a powerful message about human dignity and the right of the poor to exist, just as much as the wealthy.

CHAPTER
15

Curious Conversations
2005-07 Cameroon

So, we were in Cameroon, north of the city of Bamenda in the English-speaking part of the country. The trip was to visit the literacy programme we had been supporting from Village Aid, helping women and girls gain the skills of reading and writing needed to navigate the twenty-first-century world beyond their isolated communities. Many had been denied the chance to go to school at all, or could only read Arabic in order to recite the Koran.

But the strong contrast between the educational opportunities of the "beneficiaries" of the project and the mainly male facilitators was brought home to me one fair day when I was bumping along an unmade road in the front seat of a Toyota land cruiser. Behind me were squashed four cheerful young men, about the same age as my sons, who all worked on the project as para-legal advisers and teachers. They were all talking to each other, half in their own local language and half in English.

Then I heard the following conversation.

"No, I don't think you can call it cowardice. It was more likely post-traumatic stress."

"No, he was just paralysed with fear."

"Pretty spineless if you ask me!"

I turned in my car seat.

"Who are you discussing? What are you talking about?"

I assumed they were discussing a current situation in their country. One of them had just been released from prison, where he'd been beaten very badly and still had the scars across his buttocks.

"Oh, we were discussing Hamlet, why he couldn't revenge the death of his father for so long."

I was nothing if not stunned. Here we were, high up in the hills of Northwest Cameroon, miles from England, and I was the only white woman, I reckoned, for twenty miles around. I quizzed them about how they had learned about the motivations or otherwise of Hamlet, and learned the following.

Yes, they had studied Shakespeare in a boys' secondary school, not just *Hamlet* but also *Julius Caesar* and *Richard the Third*. There had been one textbook available, which the teacher had passed round the class with different boys reading in turn or taking different characters. None of these young men had gone on to study English Literature at university. They simply remembered their school days, and were using what they had learned about human nature through the works of Shakespeare.

I thought of my own boys back home, bright yes, and not ill-informed about the world. But I could not imagine either of them discussing Hamlet with their mates on a journey, more likely just arguing if Liverpool or Everton football teams would win the cup. This was the same year when there was a spat in the press in the UK about the decision to drop a compulsory Shakespeare play from the English curriculum at GCSE, as not "relevant" to modern life.

I have had many similar unexpected conversations along the byways of rural Africa. In Gambia I discovered an elderly man who was a huge admirer of Ellis Peters' books about Brother Cadfael, another who was a great Agatha Christie fan.

But my heart sank one time in Uganda when I asked a senior English teacher what her set books were for the Cambridge Advanced exams, (the overseas equivalent of A level still used by many African schools.) "*Silas Marner*", she replied, "That's one." Oh dear! I only hope by now, some of the hugely talented contemporary African writers have replaced old nineteenth-century British novelists.

The thirst for education in Africa remains very strong. In Ghana once, I visited a ceremony to welcome new pupils to a primary school. There are strict and very restrictive dress-codes and uniform requirements in many such schools, which often means that children cannot attend because they do not have shoes or the right bag.

But this day everyone came, correctly dressed. One young woman was starting in Class One, alongside the baby five-year-olds, correctly dressed in an adult version of their blue dresses, white ankle socks and black shoes. Even more surprising was to see an elderly man of nearly seventy in the boys' version of the same uniform. He was starting his school days, aged sixty-eight, and was wearing grey shorts like all the other male pupils.

When schooling is seen as a privilege, students will wait years, and travel many miles, often on foot to gain it. In many

Fula communities, as in Lesotho in the south of the continent, boys in particular were late being able to start school, because their childhood was spent herding cattle, and until there was a younger brother strong enough to relieve them of this tedious task, they could not start learning.

The prejudice against girls being taught in a school situation was also being gradually eroded, and I was able to witness many bright young girls being given the chance, at least, of a primary education.

If there was any hope of progressing through secondary school and even to college, it would usually depend on the support of the oldest siblings in the family.

I had one good friend with nineteen or so brothers and sisters from his father's four wives. Once the father had sent the eldest sons off to school, then he turned over the care and funding of all his younger children to their respective brothers and sisters.

Such huge extended families were commonplace among the conservative Mbororo people, where Father was treated almost as a Tribal chief, in a compound where his various wives each had their own small house, and he would often entertain in style from the main house.

I spent time with one such family, accommodated as an honorary man in the guest room of the "big" house, and walked later with the first wife, down a slippery hillside path to fetch water from a decidedly dirty waterhole. One main reason for my visit was to negotiate the rebuilding and closing in from passing animals of this water place, and lowering the ever-present risk of disease whenever its contents were consumed.

As we struggled back up the hill, and afterwards, I asked

her how she felt about being one of four wives. Wouldn't she prefer to be an only wife?

Whether she misheard me or not I'm not sure, but she said, "Oh no, I could never cope with being a lonely wife. I would never be able to do all the work."

In many ways she was correct. It was true. All the food production, growing crops, care for the children, meal preparation, carrying corn to be ground in the market, and bringing back flour, it all fell on the women.

Sometimes the younger women initially triumphed over the older, wearier sisters, but soon, once they'd had a few children, you could see their spirits fail, and eventually as widows, many "sister-wives" lived peaceably enough together, caring for each other in old age. Some fourth wives, though, were seriously bullied.

The traditional African polygamy, which by now was mainly, but not always, confined to the Islamic societies has caused much conflict. I saw this in Sierra Leone, where a younger man, without land or family money behind him would be trapped for years in a situation of powerless "youth," denied the right to farm his own land, or marry or even date the girl of his choice. The old Chief might take all the available young women for himself, blocking them from having the boyfriends and husbands they yearned for. In fact, following the tenets of Islam, and limiting themselves only to four wives had proved a discipline too hard for them.

One African friend said to me, "They always preach from the text, 'Honour thy Father and thy Mother' but they ignore the next verse at their peril, 'Provoke not thy children to wrath.'"

Veneration of chiefs stretches across many cultures. In

Northern Ghana, one woman said to me in angry frustration, "I am absolutely tired of bowing my head and almost falling into the ditch every time the chief comes by."

My younger son and I had the very humorous experience once of encountering such obeisance when we visited a chief in the Tamale area, who kept a fine horse in his small mud "palace." It wandered in and out as we met and talked to him as he sat on his throne. No-one dared remove it because it was the chief's horse, far more valuable to him than any of his wives.

Another time, in another country, visiting another chief, we were delighted to see afternoon tea, complete with china cups and saucers, prepared for us as we arrived after a six-hour journey along back roads. The kettle was almost boiling as we climbed the steps to his house.

"How did you know when to expect us?"

"Oh, they called me on my mobile phone," he replied cheerfully. I thought about this. There was no electricity for at least thirty miles.

"How do you keep your phone charged?" I asked.

"Oh, I send a boy on a bicycle to the nearest place with electricity" (which was indeed more than twenty miles away).

This chief had studied in the UK and was a forward-thinking, very liberal leader of his people, but others were by no means as happy to welcome us and our services. Education for the rural people was seen as very dangerous.

In one language in Sierra Leone, the same words used to translate "to educate" also denote the verb "to lose." If you educated your children there was a strong possibility you might lose them. This pessimism was proved right in so many cases, as Africa's most talented, brightest young people continue to try to escape poverty, conflict and personal frustration at life's restrictions.

One of the quirks of contemporary African society, which I discovered across the continent is a very loyal following to the BBC World Service. Rather like aficionados of Radio 4 in the UK, the eclectic group of listeners provides a constant appeal to lovers of the lost by-ways of broadcasting.

It is a shame that the World Service is not easily accessible to casual listeners in the UK, but if you are in Africa, the African service for many years has provided a humane platform (as one might call it these days), for retired teachers, writers, and philosophers to contribute their thoughts and news, and chat about the ways of the world. All of them speak one or two local languages, but they can share across national and tribal boundaries through the medium of English.

I listened to one report about the elections in Nigeria which was in complete contrast to the tales of mayhem and violence on the cable TV coverage. Yes, there had been a few scuffles, but according to this observer, the elections had been a huge success, and Northern Nigeria sounded for all the world like Northamptonshire.

It was a splendid rebalancing of perceived ways of reporting from Africa. Yes, there is violence, family tragedy, natural disasters and corruption, but there are also vast numbers of good deeds done, positive outcomes and small injustices removed by sane and solid citizens, just as there are in Northampton, Cheshire or even the wild country of Cumbria!

While I was in Cameroon, I had a glimpse of the danger associated with social reform, and even of talking about it. One of the young men in the jeep discussing Hamlet had been arrested and savagely beaten in custody. Pictures of his wounds were printed in the activists' newsletter and soon appeared on social media. He had to live down the nickname "Buttocks" for some time, but had been very brave. On my final day, after meeting with another group of activists in Douala, I was being driven to the airport, when we received a text message to say the people I had just met, had been arrested.

I was very shocked. "They waited till you had gone. Then someone probably bribed a policeman five dollars to arrest them, to frighten them."

"We must go straight back!" I protested.

"No, stay out of it. Someone will just have to pay the policeman ten dollars, and he will let them go with a caution. Money talks!"

CHAPTER
16

When to speak out
2003-08 The Gambia

When I first started travelling in Africa, I was ridiculously ignorant. I am still stupidly so, but I have learned a few things.

The first nonsensical thing I had to discard was the assumption that if I met with a group of people in a country, for example, like The Gambia, that all those Gambians present would:

a) Be conscious that they were Gambians first, and members of their own tribe second.
b) That they would not have foremost in their minds the power dynamics within their group.
c) That they would tell the truth, or indeed anything to rock the status quo, to a strange British woman of indeterminate rank.
d) That any of the women at the meeting would speak freely if there were men present.

I learned quickly that the right to speak, and the order in which people spoke or even simply answered questions, was strictly according to the power dynamics of the group. Understanding of local, even family politics was essential to understand if intervention from an outside body or individual, however well-meaning, was to have any hope of realising its goals. Many, many projects have failed because of a post-colonial insensitivity to such matters.

In the Philippines, which has some of the most well-trained and sophisticated community development workers in the world, this was well understood. Anyone, national or international who hoped to effect change in a community was sternly told to keep his/her mouth firmly zipped for at least the first twelve months of residence there.

I have certainly found this to be true, moving from parish to parish across the North of England, following my husband's footsteps as a clergyman. One's first impressions are usually completely wrong, and the people one expects to be the most positive and natural allies are usually the biggest thorn in the flesh. Family ties are also a given in a rural parish and you ignore them at your peril.

For a few years we lived in one of the most beautiful valleys in England, Patterdale on Ullswater, and the parish included half the lake and the mountain range round the high peak of Helvellyn. We were based there for just three years, but it was an educational experience. One small illustration comes to mind.

The village school had about twenty-five pupils, aged four to eleven, and my husband went in weekly to tell them bible stories and encourage their understanding of the Christian faith. It was, after all, a church school. There was one naughty boy who disrupted the session one day, and my husband told him off and threatened he'd have to leave the room if he continued.

"Eh, don't do that, Vicar!" complained another little bright spark. "'E's my cousin!"

"Yes, e's our cousin too!" said another voice.

"Oh, so how many of you are cousins to Billy here?", asked my husband. More than half the class put up their hands in response. And as it is in rural England, so it will be in rural Africa.

Incidentally, for those people who are interested in such things, there were several sets of twins in the school in Patterdale, just as there were as recorded by Dorothy Wordsworth in her journal when she passed a bridge at Hartsop and saw two sets of twins sitting on the wall, a hundred and eighty years before!

One thing Northern Agencies often get completely wrong is the insistence that local managers of a project do not employ their own family members, and that not to do so will be quite an understandable Western protocol to follow.

In Africa this can have disastrous results, as well as revealing the stresses within traditional culture. As mentioned above, with regard to older siblings expected to support their younger brothers and sisters in Cameroon, across Africa one of the most shameful things you can do is not support your poorer relations. If you have a decent job, why would you not try to secure a position in the company or agency for your sister's son or daughter? Crossing this barrier to "equal opportunities" will remain a challenge for years to come.

A small story will illustrate this: Village Aid had one partner agency in Gambia, where someone's cousin was on the staff, and this man had been proven to be dishonest, embezzling regular amounts of funds. A previous monitoring visitor from England had uncovered this, and left a crisp instruction to the partners that if they wanted further funding, the man should be dismissed forthwith.

The locals were alarmed, but said it would be dealt with. On subsequent applications for funding, his name no longer appeared on the wages list.

We only discovered a full year later that the local director and his senior staff team just could not bring themselves to do such a difficult thing, and had decided to simply take a wage cut themselves, to make up the salary for their cousin!

They would rather take a financial hit themselves, which none of them could easily afford, rather than confront their cousin and team member about his crime. The glue of family ties and old friendship was simply too great, and outweighed the injustice to themselves and to their own community, which he had defrauded.

But sometimes life is just too short to always give in to local culture. I have often felt this, and felt incredibly impatient observing the agony of young girls forced to go through genital mutilation because it is "culture," held up by the women's "secret societies" as if it was some weird form of freemasonry.

One young woman who befriended me in Sierra Leone was a pioneer against this terrible and widespread practice, and begged her own society to change from it immediately. Passing a law may not achieve much at first, but it certainly puts a marker in the sand, and she was working with the authorities to not only outlaw the practice, but put the law into real life.

My friend broke all the taboos by openly speaking about her experience, her pain and horror as a small girl, and the effect it had on her sexuality ever after. She headed a movement which I do hope has continued to have success. She was a very bright spark, and a brave woman.

Gaining a voice.

One way for women to gain an independent voice is to have an education. While I was its Director, and before, Village Aid's ethos was to set great store by the introduction of mother-tongue literacy, along with numeracy and the infusion of confidence about the skills that so many women had. There were many rewarding stories of the difference this could bring to a village, or an individual.

One such person, whom we could call Mariana, was a woman in Gambia whose legs were completely useless, probably as a result of childhood polio. She was confined to a battered old wheelchair, and despite having had two daughters, was seen as economically and socially nothing more than a burden on the village. She had no husband.

But Mariana joined the local REFLECT group when one was started. REFLECT is the empowering methodology first developed by Paulo Freire in Brazil, and which I had seen demonstrated so effectively in Bolivia. It uses guided self-help groups to teach literacy and numeracy, along with critical reflection. The group met weekly and learned to write words and count to twenty.

They could only manage to come together once a week, but Mariana, not fit to work in the fields growing the cassava and yams, studied very hard between classes, and within a few months had taken much further strides than anyone else. She eventually became the group leader, the treasurer of the micro-credit savings club, and then went off round other neighbouring groups, coaching them, and helping them develop their economic literacy and loan systems.

Her village realised that the person they had thought was nothing but a burden to the rest of them, was actually the person who would lift them out of poverty. It was a significant turning point for them all, and a joy to see.

Another example also came from Gambia, where the women's literacy group wrote posters and nailed them to the trees at the entrance to the village. "No girl from here marries under the age of eighteen!" they proclaimed in their own language, as a warning for marauding young men who came in search of brides. Numeracy, even being able to recognise a 7 or an 8, or understand the difference between 10, 100, and 1000 had an equally profound effect.

One woman, who had a market stall selling vegetables she had grown, told me, "When I took my takings to the local bank, the cashier would write down the sum in my savings book, but I could not understand the figures. After learning to count and recognise numbers, I realised he had been cheating me all the time, writing in 100 instead of 1000 which I had deposited, and stealing the rest. Now I can avoid being cheated!"

Another, recognising numbers for the first time, could phone her children living abroad. The world was unlocked for her.

Another, who had never possessed a book in her life, or had any in the house where she was raised, said, "I may never get the hang of reading, but I certainly understand how important education is now for my children, and I will do everything I can to make sure my kids stay in school and do well."

Poverty does dreadful things to people. In Sierra Leone I heard about a Sunday school trip arranged for young people, which needed a small amount of money to pay for the bus-fare. Some girls went out to prostitute themselves, to earn the amount needed, and no-one seemed too surprised, or shocked.

But girls across the world are now speaking up and speaking out, and some fascinating projects have empowered them both physically and socially.

Making a drama out of a crisis.

As well as learning to read and write, many Village Aid local partners encouraged role-play and drama sketches as a teaching aid. This builds on a local West African Tradition of female clowns who would often travel from village to village providing stories, often with a comic twist. There were some amazingly effective sketches and small shows put on whilst I was there. Subjects might include a conservative father's refusal to let his daughter marry a boy from a different tribe, or maybe leave the house to go to school.

Another play I watched centred on the problems facing a small micro-credit group, who borrowed money together and depended on each member making her repayment on time. The woman played the role of the defaulting debtor. She lay on the floor and screamed, "I am dying, I am dying! I cannot pay back the money!" The other cast members sternly told her, "You are in our group. Dying is not allowed!"

Role-play, managed effectively, with a sensitive facilitator, and carefully timed de-briefing, can be the most effective way to deal with contentious issues. It works as well in an African village context as in *East Enders*, maybe more so. Grumpy parents, or unjust officials can see their behaviours exposed without losing face, and just solutions can be discussed.

In my early career, I spent many hours working with schools and church-groups using the same techniques.

One role play, which always brings forth animated discussion was one based on the participants' height. I would ask the people to line up from tallest to shortest, and then take them back into Jerusalem, the day Jesus took his whip and drove the dealers out of the Temple.

The tallest were the Temple officials and High Priests, then we would work through the other groups, cattle-dealers, pigeon sellers, devout men, women, cripples and beggars, and halfway down the line, some of his disciples. After reading the story, I would ask them in their various groups the following questions?

"What do you think of what Jesus has done, and will you follow him after today?"

The results were always consistent, only the very shortest group members, (all women of course) ever decided they would follow Jesus, an accurate opinion poll on the Crucifixion, which in the Bible story happened just a few days later.

CHAPTER
17

Two taxies, twenty-six goats.
2006 Ghana

Josephine was a very bright young woman from the Eastern region of Ghana. She had applied for a Commonwealth fellowship to work within a UK agency for a few months, and, by lucky chance, we in Village Aid had applied to the same funders to receive such a worker. Josephine headed up an innovative agency in Ghana, empowering women, and promoting sexual health.

She and her colleagues would stand outside the local factory in Ghana at closing time, handing out free packets of condoms to the men who emerged. She was nothing if not brave in going to the heart of a problem and she came to join our staff.

Her time with us in Derbyshire, apart from helping her understand what British winter cold weather actually feels like, made all of our lives more interesting. When she returned to Ghana's eastern region, to take up the reins of her agency once more, I visited her there, and saw the specific problems faced by many young women, shunned by their families for having caught the AIDS virus, ironically gifted to them in most cases by their husbands, who subsequently abandoned them.

One of the schemes Josephine and her colleagues were running was to give out nanny goats to such unsupported women. The idea was to start them off on a small income-generating project which involved their goats being mated, giving birth to one or two kids, which could then be raised and sold for meat, and then returning to a good stud billy-goat to start the process the following season again. If one of the kids was a nanny-goat then it could be kept on and the herd increased.

This was quite similar to Mommy Ed's pig scheme I had seen in the Philippines back in the 1980s. In Village Aid we had run a small-scale promotion over the Christmas period, with Josephine's project as our local Ghanaian partner, and twenty-six people had sent money to sponsor a goat. So, in the spring, I went out with the cash, and we bought goats, twenty-six of them.

Matching goats to people, and seeing them go home proved a very merry occasion, one which I treasure because it cut through all the usual layers of compromise and complicated ethical conditions. I have always had mixed feelings and a good deal of worry about wealthy Northern people sponsoring individual children, though I do see the marketing need to personalise the giving. People, as they say, always give to people and animals rather than faceless organisations or progressive ideas. But sponsoring a goat didn't seem too bad an idea.

We arrived early at the yard outside a community building, and Josephine was busy writing numbers 1 to 26 on small pieces of paper and putting them into a wastebasket. I asked her what her reasoning was.

"When the goats come, all the women will try to get the strongest looking, the fittest. This way they will have to draw lots. Look, I have sticky labels which we can put on the goats ahead of the distribution. You pull a number out of the bin, and then you go and get the goat with that number. No fighting and no disputes."

"Brilliant! But how are the goats getting here? And how will the women get them home."

"Oh, they are coming by taxi!" was Josephine's very puzzling answer. "And they will have brought some rope or string for a halter. They will either walk them home, or carry them off on the local buses and motor-cycle taxis."

I couldn't wait to see this fascinating scene, and the reality was even more entertaining. The goat farmer arrived with twenty-six goats carried in not one, but two taxis. That he achieved this at all was remarkable. They all jumped out, running amok for a while, but were eventually corralled into a small section of the yard, and a sticky label with their allocated number stuck onto each goat's back.

By then a number of women arrived, mainly mothers with young children on their backs or clinging to their skirts, again on a variety of local transport, or on foot. As the meeting settled, Josephine described how it would all work. I duly said a few words, photos were taken, and the women, one by one came up and drew out a folded paper with a number on it. It reminded me rather of a church raffle in the UK. Having pulled out their number they would then go off and collect their goat. Twenty-six goats, twenty-six worthy recipients. It all ended very happily, as they made friends with their animals and pulled or pushed them towards the exit.

"Well done," I said, to Josephine and her team.

"Well, thank you and your generous supporters back in the UK," she replied. "The only problem is, I know of hundreds of women with AIDS who could also qualify for a goat."

But they do what they can. They scratch the surface, but at least they do that.

I was given a goat myself once in Ghana. She was a pretty little pygmy goat, white and in good shape, which my accompanying group of young men accepted from a chief on my behalf and pulled up onto the back of our pick-up truck. I could see they were already talking about slaughtering her and making a feast of it, but it seemed such a waste.

She was young and fertile, and would make a good little mother, an investment for the future. I also thought it was my duty – hey, she was my goat after all – to prolong her life if I could.

The driver, who was by far the poorest of all the guys in the truck, being paid peanuts, (or perhaps even in peanuts) cottoned onto my thoughts, as I sat beside him. He quietly began to suggest how well his wife could look after the goat, and how they could indeed breed from her and have her to live with their children in their little compound.

I don't normally put my foot down when being tanked round other people's countries, but on this occasion, the driver and I prevailed. By the end of the day, everyone had been converted to the idea that "Susanne the Goat" – for we had named her, which always discourages random slaughter of animals – should be allowed to live and grow up to be a productive nanny.

As night fell, and the driver finally dropped me off at my lodgings, I saw him drive away, happy, with Susanne, the little white goat still alive, and tethered safely in the back of the pick-up. I wished her a long and happy life.

Ghana is a very large country, and the regions to the south are markedly different in terms of the levels of westernisation and development to the northern regions. The north is also much more Islamic than the Christian South, and the old ways, with the power of the chiefs, and the traditional misogyny of the ancient village systems much more noticeable. The round house villages which have given people their shelter and a sense of identity could been seen from the air as we flew up to Tamale, and the gently rolling hills and deep red soil looked so peaceful from above. On the ground however, life could be very hard and very disputatious.

One particular aspect of this which impinged itself on my notice in a distressing way for my friends, is the practice of targeting vulnerable women, and occasionally men, and accusing them of being witches. This has been deemed illegal by the government in Accra, but is still prevalent across the North, where people in the villages I visited claimed the truth of witchcraft.

Very often though it was simply a money-making racket. The poor victims were sometimes tortured or even killed, but often exiled into "witches' camps," wretched areas where inadequate shelters provide some sort of sanctuary against the violent attentions of the local hoodlums and gangs. Soothsayers and shamans charge money to either "prove" the guilt or innocence of the accused, and then to take away their powers of sorcery so they can be returned to their village.

I was told of one elderly woman who was bullied by her

nephew into lending him quite a large sum of money. When she asked for it back, he refused, and accused her of being a witch. This completely innocent and previously respected woman was then thrown out of her community into virtual destitution. The nephew's wickedness was rewarded by keeping his aunt's cash, and the sympathetic applause of his friends for such a clever ruse.

The power of this belief in witchcraft also had a life-changing effect on a young Ghanaian friend of mine.

Twelve years ago, her life was changed for ever, and she was to face challenges she had never dreamed of. A very quiet, almost introverted girl from a remote Northern town in Ghana, she became engaged, to a man from an even more conservative rural family.

They looked to have a bright future between them, because he had qualified as a nurse in an Accra hospital and had secured a post in the UK, working in a large city hospital in the North of England. He worked here for a year, and even put a small deposit down on a terraced house. On a trip home, they married, and he brought her as his wife to the UK.

Ayesha spoke very little English, but they had some Ghanaian friends, all nurses, and she began to adjust to the strange culture and cold weather. As they moved into their little house, she realised she was expecting a baby, everything seemed perfect. But then disaster struck.

Her husband began to complain of stomach pains, hiding it as best he could, and carrying on working. As the pregnancy developed, Ayesha still had no idea what was to come, but by the time she was admitted into one city hospital to give birth, her husband collapsed at work and was a patient in the other one, where he himself had nursed.

Ayesha had to give birth alone, in a strange city. She had no access to money, and still spoke very poor English. Three days after giving birth to her daughter, she crossed the city by bus, and sat at her husband's bedside, to show him their baby girl as he died. He was twenty-nine, and his death was diagnosed as stomach cancer.

It was then that one of Ayesha's uncles, who knew us at Village Aid from our work with him in Ghana, begged us to go and support her through this terrible time. So it was that I have been friends with Ayesha ever since. She stayed in the UK, spending ten years in a long and often agonising battle to get residency for herself and her daughter.

"Why didn't she return home after her husband's death?" you might ask. "She had no personal right to be here without her husband's work permit." Ah, but there was one crucial reason why she had to remain, to save her own life and the life of her child. For Ayesha had been accused by her in-laws of practising witchcraft on their beloved son, who they had expected to make their fortunes by immigrating to the UK. Why would a young fit man like him die so suddenly otherwise?

As the weeks unfolded after his sudden death, she realised that his friend from university and fellow nurse, who shared the house with them, was now in touch with the in-laws, and telling them she would have access to a large fund from the Nursing Pension Fund he had subscribed to. This had indeed been the only piece of good fortune to be given to Ayesha in her sea of troubles and bewilderment, and they quickly demanded it.

The family also imagined she owned the whole house, not just a tiny 5% equity in a house, which the mortgage company quickly tried to repossess, as they claimed Ayesha would never be accepted as a mortgage holder in her own name, for she had no right to work. Had her husband taken out life insurance to cover their mortgage, the house would really have been hers, but of course, like most young men he did not expect to die, and money was very tight. She had no rights to the property, which had actually fallen in value since they had bought it.

Ayesha began to get very threatening text messages from her brothers-in-law, demanding she return, hand over her child to them, and also all the money. A village "court" in Northern Ghana, even theoretically carved out her widow's compensation money and divided it up between them, even allocating a thousand or two to the village shaman and Imam.

Eventually, partly because she was frightened for her widowed mother's safety back in Northern Ghana, she sent the in-laws more than twenty-six thousand pounds, half of her allocated lump sum. But this meant that she struggled for years on a tiny amount of money, working as a cleaner or collecting clothes to send home in containers for her sister to sell, each month paying in rent the equivalent of the mortgage payment on her little house, which is still owned, not by her, but by the mortgage company.

It was a long, bitter and often very lonely journey for Ayesha from then on. But she has a huge spirit and determination to give her daughter a future, not subject to the torture of female genital mutilation, or being branded the daughter of a witch. She was determined not to take her little girl back to Northern Ghana, under any circumstances.

She has prevailed, and in 2019, her daughter at least, was finally granted UK citizenship. On appeal to the Home Office, which had been keen for years to deport her, Ayesha was given a two-year extension in which she could legally work at last, and is now a full-time care worker, an occupation sorely needed. Ayesha's story has by no means finished, and is, of course, far more rich and multi-layered than this brief account can convey, but it is hers to share and she remains a very private person, fearful of authority, and pushed into campaigning and publicising her situation, rather than simply being a mother who wants to work and support her child.

The scourge of witchcraft accusations has been well documented by journalists in Ghana, one saying that the culture is still "beguiled" by notions of witchcraft. It reminds me of the voyeuristic inclinations of people in medieval Europe, where the almost salacious delight in reading of other people's tortures and demonic punishments was well documented.

A sharp sting of misogyny is present in so many of the thousands of similar incidents of accusing widows of their husbands' deaths, and in the asset stripping which I have seen, when a mother is left widowed. Both she and her children are incredibly vulnerable, as brothers-in-law have the right under traditional practices of coming in and removing not only her husband's land and animals, but also the very tools needed to till the soil.

The idea, I presume, was to force her to accept a lower status as a second or third wife of one of his brothers. This grabbing of women's independence, the fear that a woman who has no male "keeper" could pose a threat, is horribly common, across much of the world.

On a much milder level, the strange antipathy to widows can even be seen in the social mores of the UK and the USA. Widowed or divorced friends of mine have commented on how few invitations they get to parties or dinners on their own. They are seen as a threat to the plastic "coupledom" of suburbia.

No wonder people try to remarry, often far earlier than might be thought sensible. The dreaded thought of a woman alone sitting in a restaurant, even today, is surprisingly scary to a lot of people.

PART
FOUR

CHAPTER

18

The Street Children of Kinshasa
2012-19 The Democratic Republic of Congo

Being homeless is never easy, especially when you are six. For more than eight years I have been connected with a project in the Democratic Republic of the Congo which does its best to support the poorest of the poor in that country's rapidly expanding capital city. These are the vast population of children sleeping, working, scavenging and hurting on its streets.

Finding the children is not hard. You can walk any street after dark, look behind the market stalls, the bus station, under the bridges, in the drains, and you will see little scurrying figures, dark in the darkness. They are ragged, skinny, eyes hardened with lack of sleep and having witnessed too much violence and pain.

They are everywhere. Boys and girls, they are desperate. But they did not spring from nowhere. They have parents, family members somewhere, a history, an identity. Re-establishing their identities is often the first step in building them up as future citizens of their country.

In Kinshasa, a city of 12 million people and capital of the Democratic Republic of Congo, more than 25,000 children live on the streets. The number grows by about 3000 each year; two thirds are boys, and up to a third are girls. They sleep rough wherever they can. They struggle to find food, clothing and shelter, and a sense of being loved.

Many are sick with malaria and other illnesses, and many have suffered sexual abuse. Some street children are as young as five years old, and all are denied their basic human rights of protection, education, a loving home and the chance to thrive. The police often treat them as criminals and harass them, rather than as children needing protection.

Why so many unsupported children? The population of Kinshasa has exploded over the last two decades, from around 2 million people in 2000. Most of the growth has come from families fleeing violence elsewhere in the DRC and there are very few jobs or schemes to help them settle comfortably in the city.

Many children have lost one or both parents through illness, fighting in the country, or violent death. Others are victims of false accusations of sorcery, or shunned by a step-parent who refuses to care for the children of their partner's former marriage. Above all, dire poverty causes family destitution because of unemployment and very low earnings, which cause children to leave home in search of food and shelter.

I worked with the French based, but now international, Christian community of Chemin Neuf, and their story in Kinshasa illustrates the problem. Members from the mother community in Europe arrived in the city at the request of the local Archbishop about twelve years ago to take over a struggling urban Catholic parish in one of the poorer southern suburbs. In Kinshasa, the further your address is from the banks of the river Congo, the rougher is the neighbourhood in general.

This parish was seven kilometres south, but close to the University and not too far from the open country. You can see trees at least. Informal building, roads which a decade ago were simply footpaths, and sprawling self-build projects of houses, shacks, little shop stalls and informal meeting places have proliferated up and down the steep hills, along the riverbeds and spreading out of the city like a network of capillaries.

The people from Chemin Neuf started conversations with local leaders. What was the priority, apart from having a functioning church, and some priests to run it? The answer was clear. Above everything else, they needed a new primary school. There were hundreds of children then who had no hope of a decent education. But there was a large semi-derelict school building right opposite the parish church. If it could be refurbished and staffed, it could rise again as a decent place of learning.

So, they went to look at the school. It was certainly in a mess, but it could be cleaned, painted, repaired and refurnished. It was all doable. There was just one major problem. It was already inhabited.

More than a hundred children had made it their home, sleeping on the floors of the old classrooms and storing their belongings everywhere. If the school was to be re-opened, then these children had to be evicted, which of course would only send them back out into the open air, or into even worse situations.

It opened the eyes of the Chemin Neuf community to the scale of the problem, and they started to reflect on how to solve it. Soon they decided, the answer could not lie in building yet another planted institution like an orphanage.

These children by and large weren't orphans in the true sense of the word, some were, of course, but they were in a small minority. No, the answer lay in reconnecting children with their real families, or if this was impossible, then setting up foster placements for them, and finding a way to support the families, and foster families, so they could afford to keep the children, and send them to school.

It's a long and interesting story, but in summary, between 2008 and 2018, Chemin Neuf, with its local sister organisation, has done this amazing thing. Their local organisation, half volunteers, half paid staff, have, over the last twelve years, rescued more than 2000 children from the streets of Kinshasa, and successfully reunited them with their parents or, at least, with an extended family member, to start or return to school, and then move on to vocational training.

More than fifty street children and young people a day visit their two centres, to be fed, have their wounds and sores tended to, rest their weary little bones for a few hours, and learn how to laugh and play again. It takes totally committed staff to make this happen.

Twenty volunteer mothers, under a general manager and cook, provide a hot meal and a breakfast, and fresh clothes and washing facilities, along with one hour of compulsory literacy training each morning. This helps the children regain confidence in their ability to cope with school when they are reintegrated.

The girls' centre provides accommodation and a place of safety for girls from 6 to 13, most of whom will already have suffered sexual abuse. The boys' centre does not encourage overnight staying. The centre closes at 4 pm each day, and all the effort is put into restoring boys back to their families, most of whom can be traced eventually, by the twelve dedicated social workers who cover all the slum areas round the south of the city. Fifteen boys were staying at the centre however, some were very young and found abandoned, a few were physically or mentally impaired, some were ill with malaria or other fevers.

Family Reunification means a three-year commitment to support the families with counselling, micro-credit for the mothers to start businesses, and school fees for the child. There is very little free schooling in the Congo. Normal primary schools charge $US 100 a year, which puts it beyond the reach of the poor.

One final word: tragically many of the children end up on the street through being accused of sorcery or being witches by unscrupulous pastors of Pentecostal-style churches, who have been influenced by American missionaries to believe they can drive out demons and evil spirits by blaming children. They are then beaten, starved, even scalded or burned.

This is the antithesis of what the Holy Spirit stands for, and the Chemin Neuf community have fought vigorously to get it accepted that no child can ever be a sorcerer. This is now enshrined in Congolese law, but the battle still has to be won on the streets.

Children are resilient, and can heal from past hurts to

become educated, self-confident adults. Chemin Neuf and its friends believe that a loving family is the best place for a child, and that families can be supported to provide a positive place in which a child can thrive, organise financial support for the children to attend school and vocational training, and offer micro-credit to help mothers set up small businesses.

I had been in touch with Chemin Neuf, providing child protection and safeguarding training with a colleague who had gone there to deliver the course, but I had never been myself until the spring of 2017, when I spent three weeks on site. It was a trip and a half, but I met some remarkable children, and adults, and learned yet more about the realities of our weird and wonderfully unbalanced world.

The weather was very hot, and water and electricity were both strictly rationed. I wish Northern partners of Southern organisations would understand how hampering this is to getting reports filed on time, budgets emailed through correctly, notes taken from exercise books, scribbled in pencil and transcribed onto a laptop.

If you sit in New York or Brussels, or London, you really have no idea. I know, because I have worked as a programme manager for several large aid agencies, and the paperwork requirements never get less. I use the word paperwork advisedly though, because everything is digitised, and struggling young African managers have to leap into it or simply fail to get the necessary funding.

We live in such an impatient culture in the North that sending an email and not receiving a reply within twenty-four hours seems almost rude. But coping with everything on-line, when electricity is erratic and Wi-fi connections even harder to install and sustain, is like the labours of

Sisyphus, who had to roll a heavy boulder up a hill for eternity. Applying for large grants through the major donors in the UK, Europe or North America is a nightmare under these circumstances, enough to break anyone's spirit, because the goal is so enticing, and the means to saving years of work, as well as countless livelihoods.

Living by grant money is said to be demoralising and disempowering, but hey, the whole world does it, from the Queen downwards. Asking every humanitarian organisation to instead become a business is to ask the impossible. The poor will never be profitable.

The stone breakers

Staying in the Chemin Neuf community mother house, a mile up the hill from the two children's centres, I was somewhat cocooned in a clean and quiet compound, but on ten days out of fourteen one would find the water from the taps had dried up, and only the kindly attentions of a young man with a bucket of water from a holding tank, could enable one to wash off the grime and dust from the streets.

Writing up journals and reports was equally problematic, especially when electricity was limited to two or three house a day, often not at the time when one needed it. I realised the value of pen and paper again, if there was light to see by, and my down time was spent knitting a sweater for my grandson, which was good for me, if not for him, as it grew under me. I think he will be eleven before it fits him, by which time Paw Patrol may have lost its attraction!

Streets paved with old clothes

We walked everywhere, of course, up and down the alleyways and little lanes, linking our road with the bottom of the area where a major roundabout connected several roads going into the centre of Kinshasa. During those miles, I was confounded by something I had not ever registered before in other cities.

Many of the steps and walkways were literally paved with old clothes, shoes and other detritus which had been thrown down to stop the torrents of flood water which in the rainy season poured down the now deforested hills. A child's sock, a dress, and countless plastic bags containing unspeakable rotting rubbish were actually used instead of masonry to construct these alleys. It amazed me, the variety and toxicity of so much rubbish which formed the actual pavements beneath our feet.

The children's centres, thank goodness, had been built though with more substantial bricks. Homeless boys had themselves built their compound, under the tutelage of an elderly but committed professional builder, and this construction project had also been aligned with a vocational training centre, where I saw boys and girls learning masonry, electrical installation, and solar panel technology.

It was a relief to my poor battered feminist heart to see the girls included in more lucrative and interesting training. Yes, there was still the seemingly ubiquitous sewing room where bored girls and ex-prostitutes were encouraged to learn tailoring skills, but gender-neutral training was definitely being introduced, and even promoted.

Half the work of the staff was spent in community liaising,

and I spent a couple of days out in the communities with one of the counsellors and educators, whose role is to keep in close contact with re-homed and re-established children and their parents.

One such family may illustrate what a struggle it is. We slipped and slithered our way down several steep banks to visit a mother in a tiny cabin, surrounded by at least six children.

The woman's eleven-year-old son, the only one actually in school, had been rescued from the streets where he had been living for more than a year, simply, it seemed, because there was no room, and very little food available at home. He was now attending the local primary school, wearing the compulsory grey shorts and white shirt uniform, and black trainers, shoes being another essential if you have to go to school.

The school had fees, all schools seem to in DRC, but these were being paid by Chemin Neuf for the first year in total, and then in part in years two and three of his connection. The mother would be encouraged to start a business to keep paying them.

There was only one problem. Mom already had a job, one which took every inch of her strength and time which wasn't spent looking after her children. She would scramble up the canyon trails, slipping and sliding as we had done coming down.

She would be more sure-footed than us, but the walk would be equally dangerous, because on her head she would be carrying a large, twenty-pound granite rock. When she got it back to the little piece of flat ground outside her hut, she, her widowed sister, and as many of the children who could lift a mallet would work at the stone. The object was to crush it into hard-core, tiny pieces of stone which were used in the road building industry.

"How many hours to work this stone?"

"Twelve, at least."

"How much will you get for a sack of a hard-core?"

"50 cents, after the cost of the original stone."

"Do you do this every day?"

"Yes"

"What about the children's father? Where is he?"

She shrugs wearily.

"He comes once a year. To make another baby."

I lifted up her mallet to test it. It is very heavy. The stone was like her life, a hard, immovable jagged object which takes every bit of her strength to convert into pennies. I left them there, down their canyon, next to their cabin.

Then I remember another family, in similar employment on the road up to the multi-million US embassy in Sierra Leone, crushing stones by hand so that the diplomats can swirl past in their air-conditioned $50,000 vehicles.

The women of Africa really do carry the weight of the world on their heads.

While I was with them, and there were many inspirational hours spent with the children and the staff at the Chemin Neuf centres, it seemed a good idea to visit the British consulate in Kinshasa. So we duly travelled north.

We knew we couldn't get to see the Consul himself. He was back in the UK, but we went anyway, to talk about British Aid, and why it was so limited in this country, and mainly concentrated in the refugee camps in the eastern region bordering Rwanda and Uganda.

I realised immediately as we passed through the double security gates into the British Compound, that I was entering another world. It was a modern, well-built white building with several internal courtyards and pretty planted raised beds.

There was the sound of tinkling water, from a refreshing little fountain feature, and everything was attractive, nicely designed, quiet, an oasis away from the hurting, the pain and the streets lined with old clothes.

We were politely but reluctantly met by a very junior official, who could give us no information and no hope that the British Government could change its policies to fund our project in the capital. The actual atmosphere in the building was twenty degrees cooler than the baking hot city it served, but there was as much hot air produced inside as out.

Back down in our home suburb I had needed to change US dollars into local currency. The head of the community, an energetic young French priest called Stephen changed them for me, and explained the local money. He showed me a small very dirty red note, worth about 20 US cents.

"This will buy you a small loaf of bread, a short bus-ride, one or two stops, and, if you should want it, sex with a five-year old girl."

He was touching on the real value of the children on the streets. His words were designed to shock, and so they should. The trafficking of children for sex is a global phenomenon, and I have seen it in every country I have ever worked.

If anyone on earth are angels, they are, and the pain they go through on a daily basis is unimaginable. But it shouldn't be. We should imagine just what it means for an infant to be raped by a grown man. And the world needs to grasp the reality that for every lewd or violent act pushed onto a child, there is an adult out there happy to do it. This is what I cannot and will not ever understand.

Part of my role as a programme officer, which had first brought me into friendship with the Kinshasa project, had been to encourage them to set up the second centre, for girls. And this time it was a residential short-term home, where the girls stayed for the six weeks or so it took to try to find their families, and rehabilitate them back into something like normal family life. It often proved harder to do this for girls than for boys.

Blaming the victims of child trafficking and child sexual assault is regrettably as prevalent in the Congo as it is in England. Life in or on the streets had been very bitter for the little girls I met, who were all obviously starved of affection, and not sure how to give and receive love in any appropriate way. They clung to me and any other women they met, and hated to see us leave.

But leave I had to, and the Chemin Neuf team took me to the airport to see me off. It had been an intense and challenging visit. Maybe I was getting old and less resilient, maybe the sight of women carrying those back-breaking boulders up and down the canyons had really got to me, but a great melancholy came over me as I prepared to go through to the departure gates.

Kinshasa airport looked like an exact replica of a regional Chinese terminal, even down to the bamboo wallpaper. This was because it probably was designed and built by Chinese architects, who had simply lifted the blueprint from a previous job. But it did the business, and wonder of wonders, it had functioning air-conditioning.

The queue for check-in was long and wound itself like a coiled and messy snake back and forth across the hall. Families of various sizes with crying children were interspersed with large men in dark business suits, women in Congolese "best clothes" and just a few European NGO types, mostly, like me, looking crumpled and dishevelled next to the generally immaculate Africans.

The family in front of me consisted of a mother with several children, including a baby and a two-year-old who was crying for the toilet. She was conflicted about this and obviously didn't want to lose her place in the queue.

"C'est bien. Je serai ici avec les enfants si vous voulez aller au les bains." I smiled encouragingly. It would be a good five minutes before we would reach the front of the check in queue. The mother seemed relieved.

"Restes ici avec la madame," she said to her eldest daughter and two boys, and then added a fiercer word or two in their local language, Liguana. "Cinq minutes, merci."

The other children said nothing but seemed resigned. They were trying to manoeuvre a trolley piled high with suitcases. The family appeared to be on the move.

I wondered where they were going, maybe to join their father who might be working in Brussels or some other European city. Middle-class people, their challenges would be bad enough, but my thoughts lingered longer with the destitute, forgotten children sleeping under the market stalls and inside the drainpipes of Kinshasa. The world can be a very savage and hostile place for its youngest inhabitants.

Their mother returned, having successfully changed her baby, and we all went through the departure gates together. In Brussels, as we disembarked from the plane and dispersed through the huge terminal, we exchanged smiles, and parted, never to meet again. But we had connected. We were both mothers, women of the world, trying to make order out of its chaos.

CHAPTER
19

Blind activists
2017 Bulawayo. Zimbabwe

In 2017 I fulfilled a long-held ambition to visit Zimbabwe, as I have had friends there ever since receiving an e-mail out of the blue years earlier from a blind gentleman called Ishumael, who was the Chairman of the Zimbabwean League for the Blind. For three years or more they had been completely starved of funds from the Mugabe Government, and were looking for new partnerships.

Through the ensuing exchange of letters, a friendship began which continues to this day, but in 2015 I was asked to go myself to the country to conduct a grant assessment in Harare, and so I could link up with Ishumael, and the fee for the assessment covered our costs. He now had enough cash to take me round the country to visit some of the League's self-help groups, and schools it tried to support for the blind. The trip to the groups was inspirational, but the visits to the schools were heart-breaking.

Ishumael's own story is one about the good which can emerge from a small amount of encouragement, and of personal sponsorship, which is not something in my head I endorse, but in my heart I understand, and in my own life I have undertaken on more than one occasion.

A boy growing up in the south of the country then called Rhodesia, son of a traditional cattle-owning farmer, Ishumael caught measles at the age of six, and lost his sight as a result, for ever after. He was seen as an inevitable burden on the family, until a generous white woman who met him, sponsored him to go to what was then a good Lutheran school for the blind.

He did very well at school, and eventually progressed to University and then again to take two Masters' degrees, one in Canada, which he negotiated his way round, simply using a white stick, good manners and an excellent memory. He became a Personnel manager in a large company, married and has raised a family of six bright children, all of whom have progressed to higher education and beyond.

Ishumael told me that his brothers had once disputed whether he should inherit any of his father's cattle, as they reasoned that firstly, he couldn't physically care for them out in the bush, and secondly, they would have to support him anyway, as their blind brother.

"As it turned out," he said, "It is I who have helped put their children through college, not the other way round!"

But now the country's economy was virtually destroyed. Mines and most of the profitable companies were forced to close, and now Ishumael was driven back to using his cattle, his capital savings, sending them one by one to be sold to make ends meet. Even Visa and MasterCard had ceased to operate, and unofficial money changers were the only way to change South African rand and US dollars into the pretty worthless nominal local currency. Hyper-inflation had destroyed people's buying power.

In Harare, we met up with his friend, the then Minister for the Disabled, Senator Nyamayavo Mashavakure who was also blind, and discussed the national situation, as well as meeting the Director of Social Services, after which we set off on a fact-finding mission up and down the back roads through the Midlands of Zimbabwe.

We visited two schools for the Blind, situated in rural Zimbabwe, about midway down the country halfway between the two major cities. The first was Masvingo Primary School where visually impaired children lived in an annexe to an existing primary school. This school seemed miles off the beaten track in an area of small subsistence farms and rough scrub which would need large amounts of capital investment to make growing any crops a viable proposition.

It was a very warm dusty Saturday afternoon when we drew up. A low building with broken windows and a dirt yard greeted us. There was a washing line up behind with a few children's clothes pegged to it, but no other signs of children. Water came from a well and there was no electricity that I could see, nor any sign of human life.

Then, as we dismounted from the vehicle, a group of young children gathered round us. They were all blind or partially sighted, and three were albino, wearing peaked caps to protect their eyes from the glare of the sunshine. They were all very badly dressed and none wore shoes.

The teacher in charge, Mrs Moditta Donsa, their specialist teacher, came around the corner from an outdoor kitchen, moved forward and greeted us. She had the look of someone used to making every penny stretch to do the work of three, and gave us a guided tour of the facility, not that there was much to see.

There were two dormitories, for boys and girls, but the rooms were quite empty apart from very old iron bedsteads with thin sponge mattresses and a few cloth sheets. Several windows had holes or cracks in the panes. No pillows, nowhere to hang clothes, no comforts, toys or stimulation, anywhere.

This was home for the children, and a permanent home for some of them. The teacher told us parents sometimes paid the fees for the first term, and then abandoned the children, not even collecting them to take them home for the holidays.

"They are poor. They cannot afford to feed the children they still have at home. So, what are they to do with a blind child? That is their reasoning. It is hard for us to get them to visit or even return sometimes."

I could not imagine a more desolate and bleak existence for children, already deprived of the most needed sense. The yard where they were supposed to play had no play equipment, not even a football with a bell inside it, so unsighted children could hear where it was.

We looked at the small dining room and the menu list put up for the cook to see. But there was very little variety in the meals provided. They were mainly porridge, beans and Ugale, the maize-based thick paste, used as a heavy carbohydrate basis for most meals in Zimbabwe among the poor.

"How are you funded?" I asked.

"Parents are supposed to pay a small boarding fee, but nearly all are in arrears, and some have stopped paying altogether. We used to get money from the sponsoring Churches from the USA which originally started the school, but after Independence that eventually stopped, and they moved back to the States, so we have no external help any more, apart from what Ishumael and the League for the Blind can find for us."

Our young driver, whom Ishumael had hired for the trip, said to me quietly, "I never knew it would be as bad as this. It is quite shocking, isn't it?"

He came from a working-class background in Bulawayo but had never seen poverty like it. I unfortunately had, and was frightened that I was becoming immune to the sufferings of the poor.

Mrs Donsa explained that she was a qualified teacher of the Visually Impaired, going back to the days when things were organised better, and she had stayed on out of the kindness of her heart, in the tiny teacher's house next to the Boarding house.

This was the Boarding facility, so maybe the main primary school, a quarter of a mile away across the road and up a short hill would have more stimulating equipment to actually help these children get some sort of education. But it was as bad, if not worse, up there. The library and braille teaching facility had some elderly braille typewriters, but every single one was broken. It was estimated that a braille specialist engineer would be needed to repair them, coming from Germany and needing facilities at the cost of close to US$300 each.

The old library books had fallen into disrepair from long years of overuse, and some were by now barely more than wastepaper. It was very sad to see. All one could say, no comfort though it was, was that the mainstream primary school in which the unit was lodged had scarcely better equipment.

My short trip to Zimbabwe made me think of the country as a well-educated cultured person who had lost his/her job thirty years before and had systematically been made shabbier, and hungrier ever since. Everything was run down to the point of almost falling over, and, as usual, those who carried the country's greatest loads on their backs were the poorest. Intelligent, highly literate and cultured people had been robbed and oppressed for so long, they were close to breakdown, especially in the rural areas.

The old quasi-apartheid regime had systematically denied the indigenous population of the country of the right to live where they liked on their own land, and run their own affairs. It had been constructed purely for the benefit of the colonists, there is no doubt of that.

But what replaced it seemed little better, in terms of the rights of people to be self-governing, and the rights of children to grow up in a land free from hunger, violence and honest, equitable government. It appeared to me, very strongly, that Zimbabwe is still waiting for the government and civil society its talented and gracious people deserve.

Albinism is not uncommon in South-east Africa. By some genetic quirk it is more common there than in Europe, but for children born with the condition, sometimes called "Ghost Children," it is a cruel fate indeed. In some countries, notably Tanzania, they are savagely persecuted, with their actual body parts sought for witchcraft. The AIDS epidemic, which was misunderstood as curable through sorcery, made such superstitious savagery even more lucrative for armed gangs who seek them out. In Zimbabwe the situation is not so dire, but they are still shunned and hidden away by their desperate parents. Many wives had been thrown out for producing an albino child, accused of being cursed or bringing the birth on by infidelity or witchcraft.

The second school we visited was Musume Primary and Secondary School for senior students, and here the facilities were much better, although accommodation was still completely basic and house teachers and students shared cramped conditions. But the general atmosphere was more hopeful, and several of the young people talked to me of their hopes and dreams.

They had become blind for a variety of reasons. Measles remained a scourge, as did trachoma and poor infant nutrition, but the attitude of the students was a lesson in positive thinking. In this school, the teacher actually had a TV set in his tiny living room, so all sixteen or so of his boarding pupils squashed into it, alongside his own children, to watch a programme they couldn't see, but could at least hear.

No legs, no problem!

From the school visits we went further into the countryside. I was directed to a local guesthouse, but Ishumael and the others bunked up with friends in the area, and the next day we drove on to Mataga Growth Point where we had a meeting with a local self-help group of adult blind and disabled people, in a small hall owned by the local branch of ZNLB about two or three miles from the nearest market centre.

We arrived, a little late, as is usually the case when travelling un-made roads with drivers unfamiliar with the local short-cuts. The facility had been built with the original idea that it would be a workshop, but, of course, funding had dried up, and as usual, local entrepreneurs, especially those with a disability like blindness hadn't had the capital or business support to make use of it.

A local farmer had kept his goats inside, with the inevitable results and cleaning was urgently needed. However, there were benches and tables, and we were warmly greeted by the group leaders, who had brought some food to share.

They spoke, we spoke. I said a few words of encouragement. They prayed, and sang, and then we ate. I noticed one of the women sitting at the table was obviously sighted, and assumed she had come to lead her blind friends to the venue. It was only when the meeting broke up, that I realised this lady had absolutely no legs, none at all. Her body finished with a torso. When she left the bench on which she sat she simply jumped onto the floor and rolled herself towards the door. I was stunned into silence.

Someone asked if we could give her a lift back to the place where we had turned off the main road, two miles away, and, of course, we agreed. Three of the strongest people, because she was not a small person, pushed her up into the land-rover, and we drove her and her friend back to the village.

"How did she get to the meeting?" I asked one of the visit organisers.

"Oh, she will have pushed herself along on her bottom. It is how she's used to getting around."

"Two miles?"

"Yeah, sure."

"What about a wheel-chair?"

"Too expensive. They cost a lot here, especially one robust enough not to break on these roads."

We dropped the woman back in the marketplace, where they said her husband might come with a wheelbarrow to push her home. When I say dropped, I mean it, because when the land-rover door was opened, she literally hurled herself out, turning a somersault in the process, and landed, thankfully, heads-up on the ground below. I was in awe at her physical dexterity, and her courage. I wondered how many times she had made that leap of faith before but had landed on her head instead. She was a remarkable human being!

Back in Bulawayo, I met the other folk who staffed the Zimbabwe League for the Blind, all relying on other work or sources of income to get by. One worker was an officer in the army, blinded by a training exercise which had gone wrong. She had at least kept her job, and was a great inspiration to everyone, managing somehow to adjust to the devastating injuries she'd incurred many years before.

The sighted administrative officer, who acted as Ishumael's eyes for him, was a loyal employee as well, fitting in this unpaid work around a small shop she ran from her home. All the others were in similar dire straits but determined to keep the organisation going. However, without the central authority grant there had been no way even to pay the electricity bill and other utility bills for more than three years.

But the Headquarters was a large building, out on the edge of the city, but not in a bad area. It had originally been planned as a factory or workshop where visually impaired people could make furniture, but just as I had seen in Sierra Leone, the DRC and other African countries, hand-crafted or even small-business- produced furniture or disposable good were priced right out of the market by foreign, mainly Chinese imports.

I'd seen this twenty years before, on my first trip to Kenya, where the handwoven, virtually indestructible grass baskets had been shoved aside by imported lookalikes. The only problem was that the handwoven ones last a lifetime – I know because I still have mine and use it on a daily basis – and the sham ones wear out in a matter of months. This is of course a global problem to which there is no easy answer.

I met at the HQ with a group of spirited local blind people, again the group included a sighted person who was confined to a wheelchair with spina bifida. Her friend, who was blind, pushed her chair for her while she navigated. I asked them what they could do, what they would all like to do given say $50. And the answers were prompt and eager, ranging from food stalls, setting up a beauty salon, selling electrical components, and running a tutoring business.

These mainly younger people all had good ideas, and an ambition not to be a burden to either their family or anyone else. They knew there was no point in expecting the state to do anything for them, as there was no provision, no nets, safety or otherwise to stop them falling. Selling lottery tickets was the professional fate of most disabled people I could see on the streets of Bulawayo.

The other group of entrepreneurs who seemed to be flourishing in the city streets down which I walked were the money changers, running up and down one of the central thoroughfares, with their thick rolls of filthy lucre. I use the term accurately, because there is nothing as dirty as a small denomination note in these circumstances, changing hands many times a day. Every country needs a means of exchange, and when hyper-inflation, and lack of cash in the bank drives people onto the street, that is where the black-market flourishes. It is economics at its most raw.

My short visit to Zimbabwe ended with a most uplifting visit the next morning, a Sunday morning, to a self-help group who were meeting in a member's small house about ten miles out of town. We arrived early to the little community, just as preparations were being made. Our host was a beautiful woman in her sixties, who was becoming blind through complications caused by having caught AIDS, a condition which had killed her husband several years before. She had a productive and interesting vegetable garden, and we talked planting and growing food for some time before and after the event.

Then her neighbours and friends arrived and they sat in a circle on white plastic chairs out in the sunshine, and talked about their lives and how they worked round the problem of not being able to see. Everyone seemed to know each other and there was much joking and teasing, apart from two mostly silent men, who sat on the edge of the group and said very little. Even to me they looked out of place and I whispered to my companion, asking who they were. She hissed, "Zanu-PF spies. They always send someone along to eavesdrop and find out what we're doing, any local group which advertises a meeting."

This seemed quite ridiculous. What threat to the Party or the State would a group of mainly elderly blind people pose? But I learned it was a commonplace practice. I could see, through this simple episode, how repressive governments work, crushing the little green shoots of local initiatives in community building and co-operative organisation.

I remembered the regimes I had encountered in Latin America and in the Philippines with similar fears of anything positive emerging from the grassroots. It is especially effective in crushing the ambitions of people already marginalised and living below the breadline. What a waste of political energy.

But then a very beautiful thing happened. Within the group someone started a hymn of thanksgiving, and everyone lifted their voices in harmony and praised the Lord in genuine joy and happiness. I took a video of the singing on my camera, and posted it onto Facebook. The sullen onlookers were forced to stay and hear the blind people singing out in defiance against the darkness, against poverty, and against any feeling of hopelessness. It was a spiritually uplifting moment for me, and one I carried on with me, as I left the next day and eventually flew back to London via South Africa.

CHAPTER
20

Miracles Happen where they will

I have always been somewhat sceptical about miracles in the conventional sense, and all my reading of religious scriptures has endorsed the understanding that most stories of miracles are placed there by the narrator to illustrate what he/she believes to be a spiritual truth or an endorsement of what the core beliefs of the faith actually are. The idea that to become a Roman Catholic saint involves a qualification of having two miracles enacted after someone prays to you seems especially problematic.

But I'd like to share three very different stories which put a different slant on the matter and explore a different point of view. One of these events happened to me, and the other was narrated to me by a lovely South American Catholic bishop. The last came from a former Director of Christian Aid.

Thirty years or so ago, as I have said, I was working for the charity Christian Aid, as one of about thirty area secretaries across the country, in my case for Cheshire and South Manchester. Like all the other staff, I attended the national conference down at the High Leigh Conference centre in Hoddesdon, Hertfordshire, and during the final plenary meeting heard a call from the platform.

Was there anyone present who could accommodate two young Bangladeshi men who were on a Christian Aid scholarship to take a course at the University of Birmingham? These prospective students had arrived three days too early to register and move in to their rooms, so needed hosts for a few days.

We had a guest room, and as I had some speaking engagements lined up, I volunteered. Guests from the "South" were always welcome. One other person volunteered, so the students were divided up between us, and I escorted the young man allocated to me out to my car.

We drove the hundred and fifty or so miles home, and it soon became apparent how very homesick my guest was. Rashid had never left northern Bangladesh, not even to visit Dhaka, and the flight itself had traumatised him. He talked a great deal about his mother and how much he missed her. He obviously was suffering from acute culture shock.

"Madam, why do we keep stopping?"

"No need to call me Madam. Do you see those lights at the side of the road? When the top one shines red, we always stop to let the traffic on the other road move safely. When it is green, we can go."

"Wonderful! Of course, in my country we have no electricity, so it could not work."

I knew traffic-lights were a luxury. (In Banjul in the Gambia there used to be just one set, so famous that the location was known as Traffic-light Corner. It was an actual postal address, like another one I learned, "Behind the goalposts at the stadium.") But I wasn't sure about Bangladesh. Surely, they had some, in the cities at least.

Towards the end of our journey, I suggested that we pop into the supermarket in Wilmslow to buy a few essentials before we reached my house. My companion came with me, and stood in the middle of Sainsbury's, looking round at everything astonished.

"What a clean market! How do all the stall holders keep everything so perfectly clean?"

"It's not a covered market with lots of stall holders. It's what we call a supermarket. The shop is owned by one family. Their name is over the door, 'Mr and Mrs Sainsbury.' See?"

He was stunned into silence.

My visitor, Rashid, continued to be confounded and to confound me with his questions and the answers he received. He greeted my husband and children cheerfully, but then was obviously looking for someone else in our family.

"Where are your parents?"

"Well, they all live a hundred or so miles away."

"Do they live with other brothers or sisters then?"

"No, they all live alone."

"Alone, how can that be?"

"I don't think they would like to live with us."

This was getting a little embarrassing, and it took some explaining.

Rashid said stoutly, "My mother will always live with me, with my wife and children."

"Oh, you are married?" He had not mentioned his wife and children at all so far, and looked rather young, so this surprised me.

"Certainly. I miss them very much, but mostly I miss my mother."

I wondered how Rashid would survive the twelve months away in Birmingham, but like so many people across the world, the thirst for education, in this case a Master's degree in development economics, was a very strong driver.

The following day I had an appointment. It was mid-September and I had been asked to speak at a village school harvest festival, in a small moorland village up on the borders between Cheshire and the neighbouring county, Derbyshire. It was quite an isolated village with a small population.

I rang ahead to ask if it would be OK to bring along Rashid.

"I thought I might interview him," I said to the head-teacher, "so the children can learn a little about life in Bangladesh."

"That would be great," was the reply. "In fact, one of our helpers, a lady who comes in to hear children read, she has a son in Bangladesh. I am sure she'll be here, and I'll introduce you."

So, we went, and I helped Rashid connect with the children by asking him the sort of questions they would ask, but he wouldn't maybe have thought worthy of an answer. It all went very well and after the little harvest service, we went into another room at the school where tea and biscuits were provided for parents, guests and, of course, us. The head teacher introduced us to Mrs Weston, a sad-eyed elderly person with a kindly face. She was certainly interested in Rashid, and over a cup of tea, told him her story.

"My son, he is a vet, a doctor for animals. He volunteered to go overseas for a while with VSO and was supposed to be in

Bangladesh for just three years. But now he has met a local girl and has married her. I could not afford to go to the wedding, nor is my heart strong enough to fly. I do not think I will ever see him again!"

She was very close to tears.

"Madam, I am so sorry, but surely your son will come to visit you as soon as he can. What is his name?"

"Richard Weston."

"Richard? He is one of my very good friends! He lives in our village. In fact, I attended his wedding myself, only two weeks ago!"

Mrs Weston nearly fainted. "But look, here in my handbag I have a collection of photographs he has just sent me. Can you tell me who all these people are?"

She opened her bag and laid out the photo prints across the desk where we were sitting.

Rashid, so homesick and feeling a million miles away from everything familiar, saw his village community laid out in front of him.

He said, "Madam, your son's bride comes from a really well-known and honoured family. These are her parents. Her father is our postmaster, and these are her sisters and brothers. She is a lovely girl and your son has made a perfect choice."

I left them together, not only for the duration of the school tea, but for the ensuing evening. When I returned later to pick Rashid up, he was a happy man, and had brought great happiness and comfort to a lonely mother. Thirty years ago, there was no easy way to chat with loved ones in remote locations. Some small miracle, or collection of little miracles, had drawn a line of love between two people and given them what they needed. I still don't understand how it was possible, but it was.

An inconvenient healing.

The second miracle story I'd like to share came from another Christian Aid guest, who was invited to the UK as a partner from Brazil. He was a Bishop in a very poor Diocese, and was progressive, liberal and very involved with projects to rescue street-children from the gun-happy clutches of the police, whose reputation for shooting them was only too well known. While he was with us, we had a conversation about faith and healing, and whether it was possible to believe in it. There were so many phony charlatans around.

"Hmm," he said, "let me tell you something. Since I was a child, I have always known that I have been given a gift for healing where no other remedy seems possible. When I pray and lay hands on a sufferer, I feel electricity go from my body into that person. I can feel it, and I have indeed been able to heal people. Though I have never publicised my gift or even told many people."

This of course was tantalising. "Could you give me one example where this has happened, where you were able to heal someone?"

The shabby Bishop laughed. "I will tell you of my most successful healing! I had a very difficult Senior Bishop above me for many years. He hated the very idea of liberation theology and was determined to stamp it out. He disliked me personally almost as much, and though he could not dismiss me, because I was already in post when he was appointed, he did everything he could to block my work. He was a most unsympathetic pastor to the poor, so rarely came over into my sub-diocese.

"Anyway, one day, he did visit, and I could see the man was seriously unwell. In fact, he had cancer, and in the following weeks this became worse. He was soon confined to bed in his bishop's palace, and people feared he would soon die. I was very troubled. I knew somehow, I had the power through the grace of God to help him, but he would not thank me for it, and not believe I had any special gift to offer. I also personally disliked the man and didn't want to get the churlish and ungrateful welcome I knew I would receive.

"Anyway, I went, and it was just as I expected. He frowned when he saw me, and barely tolerated my presence. Eventually though he allowed me to pray for him, and place my hands on his forehead. Immediately I knew something positive was happening. I could feel it. He said nothing. I finished my prayers, genuflected, and left."

"And then what?" I asked, on the edge of my chair. "Were you able to cure his cancer?"

"Well, not for me to say. But he was up and out of bed, and back at work remarkably quickly, and his cancer apparently had completely disappeared."

"Did he come to thank you? Did it transform your relationship?"

"Oh, no," laughed the Bishop. "It didn't change anything. He carried on disapproving of me and blocking all the reforms I wanted to make right until he died about ten years later! I will never understand the purposes of God, and probably it is best that we don't." I have thought many times of this kindly and genial man from Brazil, and his amazingly unappreciated, and unexploited gift of healing, many times.

I heard a story of a miracle of another kind, told by a previous Director of Christian Aid who recounted a trip he had made to a very poor region of Brazil. In a remote village he was received into the home of a poor widow, who almost literally, had nothing: nothing in the larder, nothing to offer him, not even clean water. This upset her far more than it did him, as he only feared for her and her children's survival.

As they sat together on the wooden bench outside her hut, she asked him to pray with her for God to provide food for the meal she wished to give him, and he agreed, sceptical but devout. Within a short time, her son came up from the nearby river, carrying some small fish he had just caught in the stream. Then a neighbour dropped by with a small bag of maize flour. She could make tortillas. Then it began to rain, soft, clean unpolluted rain which she collected in a bowl, and they now had plenty to drink.

The weary man from England who thought it had been his duty to bring aid and hope to this distant community, exemplified by this poor widow, said it was a revelation to him. The meal, from nature's bounty and a neighbour's generosity was like a Eucharist. It fed them all and refreshed his spirit. It was a little miracle, just as potent as the widow's cruse of oil in the bible story which never gave out.

CHAPTER
21

Battling HIV stigma
2012-20 South London, United Kingdom

When I was working in London around 2012, I met a man called Ernest. The clue to his personality was in the name, although Ernest also possessed a deep and effective positivity and sense of humour, which he certainly needed. We joined forces to get funding for his small organisation, eponymously named The Ernest Foundation, because Ernest saw a need and set out to meet it.

He was a Ghanaian living in Peckham, who realised that all around him members of the diaspora West African community in London were disproportionately affected by the HIV virus, and its full-blown outcome, AIDS. These community members, for a variety of reasons, were not receiving the medical and social care available to them, and were suffering disproportionately from ill health, low self-esteem, depression and poverty.

Founded officially in 2006, but was formed several years previously by Ernest and his friends, The Ernest Foundation (TEF)was concerned about the rise in HIV infections within this sector, as opposed to the levelling out, and even fall, in other groups. It realised that this was partly due to the special cultural pressures and traditions from within the community, so the volunteers who founded TEF understood that only a community-based solution would alleviate the problem.

In the project focus area of South East London, there were 393 men, and 239 women diagnosed with HIV in 2011. In Lambeth and Southwark alone, there were 36 men and 20 women diagnosed with AIDS at the end of December 2011, and in the same year, in these two boroughs, 21 men and 11 women died of AIDS.

The larger statistics tell a grim story. 8,919 African men and 17,250 African women were being seen for HIV treatment and care in the UK in 2012, a total of 26,169. Ernest and I were especially concerned with the needs of women living with HIV and the fact that it had a disproportionate impact on African people. African women make up 68% of women diagnosed with HIV, and are estimated to make up 65% of all women living with HIV, both diagnosed and undiagnosed.

Based on my previous work with women in Ghana and Sierra Leone, I had a special concern with the diaspora groups in London, and wanted to support Ernest. Between us we managed to get a Big Lottery Grant which kept his work going for three years and through meeting up with Ernest and his group leaders on several occasions I had an insight into the particular troubles faced by those people.

I also took on the role of monitoring and evaluation consultant for him, along with my son Chris. As part of this process we had regular feedback sessions to the peer group meetings, training and therapy sessions which he organised, and the voices of the participants came through very clearly.

"I was very depressed, and I couldn't talk to anyone."

"The way they looked at me, I didn't find comfortable."

"I was so frustrated with my life."

"I was worried about the reaction after telling my family."

"I felt very isolated."

The most frequently quoted reasons for coming to group meetings were the opportunity to make new friends, to feel safe from criticism and to enjoy the camaraderie of a shared meal.

"The foundation has really helped me get on with my life."

"I like this group because it's like one family. The coordinators are very friendly; they make everybody feel at home."

"The staff and volunteers are very committed and helpful."

"The group has helped boost my confidence and recently I have started IT training."

"In the summer I enjoy the trips to the seaside, from there I'm happy and stress free."

"I have met a lot of people here and made many friends. Friends always check on me and visit me."

"We give each other peer support which is very important"

Many members talked about how happy they are to receive a meal.

"The food last session was good!"

"They always make sure we eat."

"I enjoy the food. We eat every time we meet."

"They make sure we obtain help even from the food chain."

Ernest's programme was initially devised by and for people from a West African background, and this contextual reality provided both a strength to the programmes but also a constraint, in that tribal or national self-consciousness remains high among the African diaspora communities in London, and people appeared to easily feel shy and isolated when mixing with groups of other backgrounds.

Ernest's approach was very much based on peer support, and also inclusive training and information sharing for those people who were brave enough to admit they were HIV positive and start to attend meetings. The cultural taboos on the subject came from their home situations back in West Africa, and initially many people, especially women, were very scared of admitting their positive status.

Ernest could see the reasons why people were reluctant to talk about their health issues. He had a practical idea of laying on a good hot meal at the end of each meeting, with food the people would enjoy from West African recipes. This really drew in the folk, who often sorely missed the traditional spiced meals of home.

Ernest decided to organize days out, hiring a bus and taking people outside London to parts of the country they had never dared visit before. These days out, including a trip to the seaside were often mentioned as a real treat, and built confidence in travelling outside their own neighborhoods. Even coming to the groups from some distance has been character building, if problematic, because of the cost of travel.

I realised just how tight the lives were, lived by some immigrant people in London when I talked to an elderly volunteer who was acting as a receptionist at one meeting. She shared with me that she lived in Peckham, and occasionally went as far as Lewisham, the neighboring borough, "to go to the department store."

But, and this truly amazed me, though she had lived in

London since coming from Jamaica in the 1960s, she had never crossed the River Thames, never walked round the West End and seen the historic centre of the capital, never visited the Houses of Parliament, Piccadilly Circle or walked down Oxford Street. Such freedom to explore what was surely her own city she didn't claim.

She was trapped by her own expectations of what people would think if she dared to go north of her own boroughs. I had come down from North London on a direct bus route from outside Waterloo station. It only took about fifteen minutes, but for this lady, it was a journey to another world.

The majority of people of African descent with HIV in London hail from East Africa but the West African communities, especially Ghana, are less able to be confident about their HIV status. As the programme has developed, TEF sought to break down barriers between tribal or national groups, and be truly inclusive. It was challenging itself to reach out across the board to other ethnic groups, and to the gay community. Only two support group members self-defined as gay in the support groups.

Another challenge was the extreme poverty of those attending the groups, 85% of whom are unemployed. Because of this, many are living below the poverty line, whether in work or not.

Education played a large part in Ernest's strategy. Anecdotal evidence from group members certainly did show much increased knowledge of HIV and its related therapy, through his classes and lectures from guest health professionals and psychologists.

The level of knowledge evidenced by quizzes and tests improved. People also reported better health and wellbeing (we were told that two people became engaged to each other through the groups, having learned about the way to have safe sex while HIV positive, and finding that love and happiness were within their means).

TEF also manned information stalls with fliers, information sheets and other factual material, at markets, public events and in public places. This outreach needed great self-confidence and bravery and, in its turn, improved the morale of those who took part, as there was no negative response or hostility shown to the messages being put out. Assemblies and classroom sessions were held in three secondary schools, with annual return visits requested. More than 500 young people were reached and responded positively to oral question and answer sessions.

Ernest and I tried again and again to get further funding for his programme, but without success, so the blooming of self-confidence, better health and the increase in happiness it gave to its participants was a short springtime. But it taught me some extremely valuable lessons, one of which was the debilitating nature of isolating people within ethnic communities, and language groups, and the simple liberation felt when you can join a peer support group and actually feel you have a voice to express who you are and what you feel.

CHAPTER
22

The Importance of the story
Told from a context

I had seen the power of giving a voice to the voiceless all over the world, as my son did as well when he travelled in Nepal and talked to women there, whose lives were constricted by an aggressive patriarchy which normalised wife-beating and bullying. Is it so great a demand that men and women should be able to speak out and have confidence in themselves and their own needs and hopes?

Poverty and the extreme inequality of resources we see in our world today is a cruel constraint on people's ability to thrive and grow and meet their potential. When you starve a child, you starve a country of its future.

While I worked at Village Aid, there was what I thought a frankly ridiculous idea by a TV company to take a middle-class British family and drop them into an African village for a short period of time, to see how they and their neighbours got on and related to each other. A call went out to development agencies to see if we would like to recruit both the African village and the British family. Anyone with a modicum of knowledge about life in Africa could see the possible pitfalls to this notion.

One thing I could see which would take away any idea of reality, was the general level of health and prior education of both parties.

In many poor African communities, a girl might undergo female genital mutilation at six, often causing years of pain and blood loss. Then she would have been married at twelve or thirteen, and by the age of twenty would probably already have had six children, possibly several miscarriages as well, and be chronically anaemic and permanently exhausted.

But she would know how to farm a hectare of land to feed her family, and how to carry gallons of water for several kilometres on her head every day. She would know how to build and thatch her hut and plaster its walls with mud. She would know how to cut the jiggers out of her children's feet, and how to pound manioc or cassava for hours on end in order to achieve the food in a diet very high in unrefined carbohydrate to keep her family from starvation.

She probably could not read or write much, if at all, but she would have in her head all the knowledge passed down by her mother and grandmother. She would be able to sleep on a bare earth floor, covered with only a thin straw mat, and she would be able to assist her sisters and friends as they gave birth in the same hut, in the same condition. She would know the old songs and dances, and the funeral rites, but her ways were not those of western educated people, and her physical strength would be tested to the limit every day. A British mother would have a completely different set of skills, and life experiences.

I watched another TV documentary once where bosses

from the UK were filmed as they tried to show people in Africa how to achieve a higher standard of living and live more "efficiently." The camera crew followed one British project manager who was determined to build a community centre or school in a remote village, and decided that the local men just needed organising properly for this to work brilliantly.

"I'll see you all here tomorrow at 8 am sharp," he instructed the assembled group. But the next morning, no one arrived on time. He was furious, and when they did arrive, much later, demanded to know why the men had not kept to his schedule.

There were several reasonable excuses, but one man said simply, "We did not come, as none of us knew when 8 o' clock was. We do not have any clocks or watches among us." The manager had to rapidly think again about a lot of his assumptions. The documentary never said if the school was ever built.

Nowadays, of course, technological advances have indeed transformed much of Africa, especially in the urban areas. Like the rest of the world most men and older boys have a mobile phone to hand, and children working away rely on such phones to talk to their parents back home

Internet cafes are everywhere these days, but I heard one very depressing fact, that most young people were found to be spending their precious coins not improving their minds with fact-finding, nor applying for jobs, but simply looking for pornography.

But in the rural areas of much of southern Africa, life has not changed much in the last eighty years, and in some cases, especially where climate change is driving people right to the edge, poverty is increasing, and lives are harder and more precarious for people and animals alike.

As much of this book has been predicated on a British, liberal-minded and culturally entrenched Christian view of the world, I thought I might include one final, rather mysterious story, one about a visitor who came to see us when we lived in Patterdale, high in the remote fell country of the English Lake District.

It was two days before Christmas, the mountains around us were covered with snow, and soft curtains of frost hung over the yew trees in the churchyard, making them stand like hoary ghosts between the warmth of the Vicarage and the icy sanctity of the Church.

My husband went over early in the morning, to open the door to let in the expected local young men who enthusiastically liked to swamp the inside of the church with a virtual forest of green fir and spruce, even yew, cut from the surrounding trees, for the Christmas season.

Inside the church porch, however, he met a man, so cold he was almost frozen solid. He had been sleeping rough, and by golly, he must have been tough not to perish in the night. David, at first, took him into the church and thawed him out a little on the radiators, then when he could actually walk again, brought him back to our kitchen, where I was feeding porridge to our two small sons.

Our surprise visitor sat by the Rayburn and while I cooked him some breakfast, porridge, boiled eggs and toast, he told us his story. He came originally from Cornwall, Redruth, in fact, where he had lived quietly with his mother in their council house. When she had died, the house was taken back, as his parents had been the notional tenants, so he had set out to find work and a new home.

He was hard-working and willing, but he was what our

present Home Secretary, Priti Patel, likes to call "low-skilled," and in those days casual work sufficient to feed and clothe and house a person was hard to find. So, he simply kept walking north, always optimistic, always cheerful, but gradually the summer turned to a cold, wet autumn, and then to winter, with long dark nights, when many doors were firmly shut against him.

Somehow, by blind chance he had ended up hiking down our remote and isolated valley. He had called the previous day at several of our church-going parishioners' houses, asking if they had any small jobs in return for a meal and maybe somewhere to sleep, but no-one had taken him up on that offer. Ours was the first house to open its doors, but of course it was the Vicarage, where we were used to strangers and not fazed by casual callers. He wrapped his cold fingers round a mug of tea and looked happy.

It was two days before Christmas, and I felt we should offer him hospitality for the holiday. But my mother and my father-in-law were both expected in a couple of hours to arrive and stay with us, as they always did for the duration of the next two weeks, and they had both often expressed their opposition and alarm at our casual attitude to strange houseguests. What would they think? Anyway, would it really be wise to take him in over the holidays, which would make a very long weekend?

The outcome, as expected, was not one I am proud of. We fed the man up, looked up the times of opening of the Benefits office up in Penrith, and when the next bus was due to make the twelve-mile journey, and politely told him to leave after breakfast. He, equally politely, agreed to go promptly, and did his best to hide his disappointment.

"Would you like to wash and shave first?" asked my husband, and showed him upstairs to the bathroom, where the man enjoyed the hot water, soap and towels. Then, eventually, he slipped away out of our lives for ever, back into the frozen mysteries of our lakeside Cumbrian valley. It was two days before Christmas, and the weather was closing in.

Later, when I had time, I went up to the bathroom to tidy up. There was nothing to do, except to sweep up all the straw which had fallen from his clothes. He had been sleeping in a stable, obviously. I understood then that the quiet man had very likely been an angel, sent to proclaim the gospel of the Incarnation, but we had not made room at our inn. Boiled eggs and a mug of tea hadn't really cut it somehow.

While we are on the subject, the eggs laid by our hens have sustained many an unexpected visitor to our houses, nineteen in all, over a lifetime of moving home. After not letting the Christmas visitor stay, I repented, and generally always tried to provide open-hearted hospitality. When we lived in Patterdale, things did get slightly out of hand, as we were directly on the Coast-to-Coast hiking trail, and forty-two separate visitors came overnight to stay during our three years there. Having come from a university chaplaincy, we did at least know most of these travellers. But there were many later people on the road, or homeless, or living in a bus shelter, who sat at our various tables.

One of them, Mary, was, however, just too dirty to have in the house, as she refused to wash, or part with any of her various layers of clothing, most of which were deeply infested. We would therefore sit out on the garden bench in the Vicarage in Ellesmere Port, and I would bring her tea and sandwiches outside.

She always talked of her dream of moving over the water to Liverpool, where she said the Sisters would care for her. But even though I recklessly offered on several occasions to drive her there myself, she refused. It was a dream, and she wanted to keep it that way. She lived on Gold Label strong ale, which she kept in the pockets of her man's overcoat, and on her illusions of the Nirvana of that convent in Liverpool which would one day take her in, just not right now.

We would talk of many things until the wind grew chilly, but the only thing Mary would avoid discussing was her own past, whether she had had any children, or been married once upon a time.

"I had better get on," I would eventually say, standing up and encouraging her to move. "Sorry, Mary, I have the ironing to do."

"Och, don't you just hate ironing?" she replied, very sympathetically. "Of all the household jobs, it's ironing that I just can't be doing with!"

Bless her. Mary had not been inside a house, I reckoned, for at least twenty years, probably more. She slept, when she was in our town at least, in a bus shelter on the Chester Road. Years later, after we had moved away to another county, we heard she had been killed, falling in front of one of the buses after too many Gold Labels. She was a real person, and I called her a friend.

CHAPTER
23

Hard truths spoken
In an unfair world

The man covered in straw, and Gold Label Mary, visited us many years ago, but they, and many other visitors like them, remain clear in my mind. As my children grew, and we moved round the UK, the restlessness which I had first felt as a child in the Cotswolds stayed with me, and I decided to work for myself and make more time for writing. I achieved the first, but the second has only recently come to fruition. Yet all through my working life I must have completed hundreds of thousands of words, in reports, assessments, and fundraising bids. They served a purpose and have now floated out into the ether.

After working for both large and small non-profit agencies, and also venturing into the field of education for six years or so, in 2008 I decided to go freelance as a consultant advisor in international development. This change of pace led to a decade of work when I interacted with more than two hundred different organisations across the world. Much of this was made possible by the "magic carpet" ability of the internet to connect us all within a second or two. It is one argument for the power of prayer, if humans can achieve this without any divine support, then how much more powerful might one's communications with God, the Goddess, or other higher beings be.

By the mid-2000s you could easily talk to people on screen as though they were in the same room, and I made and kept many friendships with people in Africa and India through Skype. I conducted so many assessments and evaluations that I felt I knew people personally, even though we will never meet.

But I did have many personal encounters as well, and developed a huge respect for people working all across the not-for-profit sector everywhere in the world. I was asked by different organisations to conduct health checks on charities and agencies, and became an old hand at assessing their viability and essential ability to run projects which did help the people they were supposed to be supporting.

Much is made by right-wingers of "aid" going astray, and people have a common tendency to assume that amateur, small scale charities are somehow a better recipient of donations than large ones. This is a paradox much loved by the Tory media, who don't warm to the idea of professional fundraising to help the poorest of the poor, but which also promote a business-oriented approach to all and sundry, urging people without boots to start depending on their own bootstraps.

I have seen this played out in so many different scenarios. Mothers of the world are urged to start small businesses, and so sit on traffic islands and dirty street corners selling vegetables and home-grown fruit for a few pennies. Microcredit training and the associated loan schemes are attached to nearly every project involving women across the world.

The market is brutal and loves no-one, however. Small children try to sell hair ribbons to people emerging from cinemas at midnight, and everywhere, in every continent, infants are traded for sexual gratification and the disgusting predilections of depraved adults.

There are many better ways to help people live lives of dignity and reach their potential than this, but they would take serious investment, not projects aimed to boost the businesses in the donor countries, or cement ties with dictators.

It's a tough call. I can bear witness to the truth that keeping track of large amounts of money, and I am talking tens of millions here, needs astute and well-trained accountants and auditors, who don't come cheap. It also needs hardened old cynics like me, who can smell a rat at twenty paces, and who have learned not always to believe what we are told.

However, and this is very important, that isn't all. The old proverb about not blaming the man who steals the goose from off the common, but rather those who stole the common off the man, is a bedrock narrative for why money goes astray. We spend disproportionate amounts of time and money pursuing benefit claimants who miss an appointment, or over-claim by £100, while ignoring the tax avoiders, off-shore account holders and hedge-fund managers who bet on misery. The 2019 film 'The Laundromat' taught me that, exposing the scale and power of such blatant corruption.

The rich and powerful of this world will always stay rich if they control the capital, the land and the means to production. Aid money given to the best independent agencies is rarely lost to corruption. Governments feeding their cronies in other suspect regimes, this is where money is far more likely to be lost or wasted on vanity schemes.

In my own, not entirely limited, experience, I have seen the human spirit rise up and dance in the most unpromising of places as brightly and excitingly as I think it ever could. The Thomas Hardy poem about the man breaking clods in the face of warfare and carrying stoically on through the world's chaos still contains a valuable truth, and the essential mystery of life remains elusive.

But similar messages and messengers surround us constantly. Whether it is the opening of a crocus flower through a concrete street and in the face of an icy North wind, or the sweet smell of a baby nuzzling against its mother's breast, these fragments of glory provide cyphers into a world of mystery and miracle we are still nowhere near comprehending.

Words are constructed by people, whether in prose or verse. Poetry, just as much as physics or business studies, can help us understand what it means to be human. The thousands of people have crossed my path, or allowed me to cross theirs, and left me their stories, taught me their songs and shared their heartaches and happiness's.

These "other people," have given my life much of its meaning, and are a bulwark against the ever-present tendency to despair, as we all might, in the face of cruelty, pain and needless suffering. I thank them all. This book is written for them, the people squashed at the back of the bus. They are the people to whom the decision makers should listen.

CHAPTER
24

Epilogue related to a 'virus'
In a world-wide pandemic

We are living in a very strange time, a time when the world has been brought to a global gasp of surprise and a realisation that, whoops, something we had almost forgotten, human beings actually belong to the same species. Chinese, Russian, American, African, we are all in this together. None of us can live in isolation, or in exclusive tribes. The whole world will now surely fail or heal together.

And also, we have perhaps learned that we might now need to withdraw from the headlong rush towards consumerist frenzy, to protect the vulnerable, to support the weakest, and use the world's resources more carefully, and more fairly. In addition, it has been brought home to us that those people who were thought low-paid and therefore low-skilled are in fact the bedrock foundation people of our society, vital to our survival, far more important than hedge-fund managers, footballers or celebrities.

The famous American anthropologist, Margaret Mead, maintained that the most important archaeological find ever made, was of a healed human femur, the biggest leg bone. This indicated that the person it belonged to, had been helped to heal and recover from a devastating injury. Animals with broken legs never survive in the wild. It was the first indication of a caring society, where a person was nursed back to health, where he or she was fed, protected, carried, until they were well again.

I believe we retain to this day, the same impulses of a shared humanity. We do care, we do believe in kindness, and justice, and fair play. So, let's use this time wisely. Let's exercise the often-underused faculty of critical reflection, our wells of kindness and compassion. Let us realise how wonderful is our shared humanity. And above all, let's not fear the worst, but hope for the very best, and let's go to the back of the bus, and travel with the people we will find there.

Pickering April 2020.

Appendix 1
Making shoes in Bangladesh

(This extra chapter has been contributed by Christopher Garnett, my son.)

Making shoes in Bangladesh is so easy a child can do it. That's what I found out while touring Bhairab's shoe factories, with a programme officer from a local charity working to rescue children from this slavery.

The acrid smell of glue and burning rubber hit me straight away. Peering through the door of the first factory, I could just about make out five young boys sat on the floor staring at me. Slipping my shoes off, I entered and spoke to the youngest. With Mohammad translating, the boy told me he was just eight years old. I asked him until what time he was working.

"Two or three am sir," he replied.

Mohammad explained to me that after Ramadan shoe sales surge. Once Ramadan is over, everyone wishes to dress smartly and wear new shoes. In order to meet the demand, it's not uncommon for children to work two shifts each day.

Many children become very ill after the Ramadan period due to exhaustion and weakened immune systems.

He went on to explain how the process of shoe making is not so complicated, that's why children can be employed. Each child has one designated job: one may cut the soles, or may be doing the gluing. The lack of ventilation was the most obvious hazard, with no windows and no fan. If the factories do have fans, they are often broken or aren't working due to regular power cuts. The factory owners also turn them off during the gluing process in order for the shoes to dry better.

Many "factories" are no bigger than twelve feet by twelve and can be more accurately described as small workshops. Children as young as six work in the factories or their own homes, facing hazards that include contact with harmful chemicals and sharp objects, working for long hours under poor lighting in cramped and unsanitary conditions. If that wasn't enough, they also have to operate hot and heavy machinery and carrying burdensome loads.

Trying to motivate parents to take their children out of the shoe factories and into school is one of the most challenging aspects of POPI's work, bolstered by various initiatives to support parents and replace their children's income. One of these initiatives is to provide small low interest loans.

Many of the parents have increased their average monthly income by 30%, equivalent to 300 BHT or around £3. Ask people in the development sector what they associate with Bangladesh and they are likely to answer "natural disasters and micro-credit," particularly since Mohammad Yunus was awarded the 2006 Nobel Peace Prize for his Grameen Bank. Bangladesh has a remarkable development sector and there are hundreds of micro-credit institutions.

But the scale of the task is overwhelming and the demand for micro-credit far exceeds supply. Bare footed children wander the narrow passageways outnumbering adults by a considerable margin. Almost 50% of the local population are under the age of 18 and it's not uncommon for each child to have at least five siblings. No parent wants to expose their child to life-threatening environments but the stark fact is that many have no choice. POPI alone cannot provide all the answers.

After visiting three more factories whose owners are still to be persuaded to stop employing child labour, we went to one where the owner has adopted the safe practices POPI are promoting. This project, known as the Sustainable Elimination and Prevention of the Worst Forms of Child Labour or SEPWFCL, aims to reduce child labour in Bhairab's shoe industry. Propaganda posters covered the walls, advocating the abolition of child labour and listing all the requirements of a safe working environment.

To date, POPI have successfully released 500 children; 400 of them are attending the catch-up schools. Encouragingly, the other hundred have now progressed to mainstream schools. The grant received from Comic Relief has proved successful and I hope many others follow POPI's lead.

But with 6000 shoe factories still employing children in Bhairab, without practical and comprehensive action from the Bangladesh government, organisations such as POPI can only make a small difference when big change is needed. Eight-year-old boys shouldn't be gluing shoes at two am.

Child labour is a visible part of everyday life in Bangladesh. Children often work in jobs that are hidden from view, such as domestic work, which makes monitoring and regulation difficult. According to UNICEF, Bangladesh has a workforce of 7.4 million children aged between 5 and 14. On average, children work 28 hours a week and earn 222 taka (3.3 USD) a week, a pathetic wage hardly commensurate to the labour they put in.

Visiting a cigarette factory, I witnessed girls as young as five rolling cigarettes for the local market. Other examples of child labour include welding, working in brick factories and in auto workshops. Working from an early age impedes the children's physical growth and intellectual and psychological development, which then also has negative effects on their long-term health and earning potential.

Children are mostly vulnerable on account of physical immaturity and the exposure to unsafe workplaces. Nearly all child labourers (something like 90% of them) are affected by physical pain during working hours or afterwards. What makes the situation worse is that most of the child labourers get no professionally-recognised treatment of their health problems.

Bangladesh's 421,000 child domestic workers (three-quarters are girls) face particular vulnerabilities because they work behind closed doors. Almost all child domestic workers work seven days a week and almost all of them sleep at their employer's home, meaning that they are completely dependent on their employers and often have restrictions on their mobility and freedom.

Over half report some kind of abuse during their work, such as scolding or slapping. Levels of exploitation are also extremely high, as indicated by the fact that more than half receive no wage at all. Instead, they receive benefits such as accommodation, food and clothing – further reinforcing their dependency on their employer.

Hundreds of thousands of Bangladeshi children work in hazardous jobs. These are jobs that have been identified by the ILO to expose children to hazards including: physical, psychological or sexual abuse; excessive work hours; an unhealthy environment. For instance, 3,400 children work in brick/stone breaking for the construction industry. Working children often live away from their families in situations where they are exposed to violence, abuse and economic exploitation.

Their vulnerable situation puts them at risk of trafficking as they seek a better life for themselves. A rapid assessment survey of commercially sexually-exploited children showed that half worked in other sectors before being lured into sex work. Additionally, more than half had been forced or trafficked into the industry, enticed by false promises of jobs or marriage.

The life of a child sex worker is even more one of violence, exploitation and physical and psychological health problems. The majority of child sex workers are depressed and three-quarters of them had been ill in the three months before the rapid assessment survey took place, many with sexually transmitted diseases. In the 3-12 months prior to the survey, one-quarter of the children were beaten, and another quarter were raped.

I returned from Bangladesh with the voices of those children still in my ears. The pitiful amount they earned, making shoes, scraping fish, working in the brothels, would always be a price too high for the destruction of their childhoods. They deserved so much more. Maybe in the future, people will look back in horror at the things we accept today. I certainly hope so.

Chris Garnett.

Acknowledgements

Many people have helped me write this book. Firstly I would like to thank all those mentioned in it, whose stories have enriched my life and given it meaning. Their contribution has been invaluable, more than I could ever repay.

I would also like to thank many friends who have read the various versions of the manuscript and helped edit it, and also iron out those little typos and stupid glitches along the way. I need to especially thank Jane and Richard Inglesby, Revd Richard Jackson, Earnest Nkrumah, Ishumael, Gaynor Pollard, Antony Pritchett, Sue Richardson, Annabel Strachan, and Linda and Romy Tiongco.

I would also like to thank my professional editor Susan Cahill, who first encouraged me with her enthusiasm and her skills at helping me shape the narrative, and Marcy Pusey who has unpacked the mysteries of self-publishing for me so clearly. I would also like to thank the designers at "100covers" who have provided the cover design. Brilliant work, guys!

Finally, of course I thank my family, David, Chris and Tim, who supported and encouraged me through all the many journeys I took away from home, and through the hours I spent burrowing away in my office. Without their help not a word of this book would have been written at all.

Follow up suggestions:

If reading this book has made you want to do something practical in response, then please consider supporting either Christian Aid, www.christianaid.org.uk, or Village Aid, www. villageaid.org.uk. I can guarantee that in both these charities, any money will be very well spent, and reach the people who need it most.

FINALLY: If you enjoyed this book, then please leave a review and recommend it to your friends. This can make a huge difference

D17

Printed in Great Britain
by Amazon